Wicked Palm Beach

WICKED PalmBeach

LIFESTYLES OF THE RICH AND HEINOUS

ELIOT KLEINBERG

THE
History
PRESS

Published by The History Press
Charleston, SC 29403
www.historypress.net

First published 2009

Cover design by Marshall Hudson

Manufactured in the United States

ISBN 978.1.59629.794.4

Library of Congress Cataloging-in-Publication Data

Kleinberg, Eliot.
Wicked Palm Beach : lifestyles of the rich and heinous / Eliot Kleinberg.
p. cm.
ISBN 978-1-59629-794-4
1. Palm Beach (Fla.)--History--20th century--Anecdotes. 2. Palm Beach (Fla.)--Social life
and customs--Anecdotes. 3. Palm Beach (Fla.)--Biography--Anecdotes. I. Title.
F319.P2K55 2009
975.9'32063--dc22
2009026266

Contents

Contents

Introduction

"HYPOCRITE'S ROW"

During Prohibition, the Royal Poinciana Hotel in Palm Beach featured a secret hallway that people could employ to sneak to a private area where they could drink. It was called "Hypocrite's Row."

Few eras in few places are as exciting, outrageous and tragic as the period between the end of World War I and the hammer fall of the Great Depression, when Florida partied, passed out and woke up with one heck of a hangover.

Enjoy these tales, most of which originally appeared in the *Palm Beach Post* as full-length features or segments of my "Post Time" local history column, which marked its 500th segment in August 2009 and was the basis for my first History Press book, *Palm Beach Past: The Best of "Post Time"* (2006).

The Depression, of course, didn't shut down the party; it was just on hiatus. It would be a world war, of all things, that restored prosperity to the quiet state at the end of the line and started a population explosion that continues today.

And, of course, the wickedness never ended. Did you really think it would? Welcome to Wicked Florida!

I

Wicked Tales

The Last Hanging

"Whiskey and Bad Women Were the Cause of It"

In 1923, the Florida Department of Corrections began conducting all executions by electric chair and centralized them at the state prison in Raiford. Before that time, counties had carried out the penalties themselves.

The last such death in Palm Beach County is believed to have occurred on July 2, 1915, when Shelby Wise was hanged at the county jail on First Street in West Palm Beach.

Wise had stabbed another man in Reno, the neighborhood along the railroad tracks near Banyan Street that held some of the city's most notorious whiskey dens and brothels.

Claude Brown, who ran a packinghouse in Boca Raton with his brother, had come to West Palm Beach on Saturday night, April 12, 1914.

Sometime early Sunday, Brown was at a prostitute's home, arguing over money and drinking. Witnesses said that Brown struck Wise, who lived with the prostitute, in the face with a bottle. The two scuffled, and Wise stabbed Brown four times.

A railroad worker found Brown near death along the track. Someone said that Wise had left town, heading north. Two deputies gave chase. About six hours later, they found Wise eight miles north of town.

At the trial, prosecutors argued that the time between Brown striking Wise and Wise chasing him made the murder premeditated and worthy of the death penalty.

Race was a far more visible issue in South Florida in 1914. Brown was white; his killer and the prostitute were black. Wise's defense attorney asked the jury not to be influenced by race. He said that Brown was the aggressor and asked that Wise be convicted only of manslaughter.

Shelby Wise, believed to be the last man executed in Palm Beach County before the state centralized executions, smokes his last cigarette before his hanging, held on July 2, 1915, at the Palm Beach County Jail on First Street in West Palm Beach. Standing on the scaffold (order not known) are Palm Beach Sheriff's Office captain George Baker, Deputy George Baker Jr., Deputy Bob Baker and Deputy A.P. Gore. *Historical Society of Palm Beach County.*

On June 26, 1914, after deliberating for two and a half hours, a jury found Wise guilty of first-degree murder.

"Hopeless, no possible chance for life, the prisoner sat with downcast eyes," read a June 26, 1914 story in the *Tropical Sun*, a predecessor to the *Palm Beach Post*. "From not one face left in the courtroom did he read a sign of mercy, showing plainly that for him, death had already begun."

Wise spent his time in jail singing gospel songs and preaching to fellow inmates and even the press. "My soul is right with my maker, and I am ready to die," he told reporters.

"Whiskey and bad women were the cause of it," Wise said of Brown's murder. "Indeed, I am sorry. But then, it is all over. And I am not worrying about it anymore."

At the county jail, on First Street in downtown West Palm Beach, work on the scaffold began. Governor Park Trammell delayed the hanging by two weeks to let Wise's lawyers appeal for a lesser sentence. But the state's

Shelby Wise after his hanging. *Historical Society of Palm Beach County*.

pardoning board turned Wise down. When he was told of his fate, Wise smiled and said, "All right."

On the morning of July 2, Shelby Wise smoked a cigarette on the scaffold and then stood as deputies placed a black hood over his head. The lever was pulled, and he fell through the trapdoor.

Originally published in the *Palm Beach Post*, December 21 and 28, 2005.

The Death of Martin Tabert

"He Saw the Bad Part"

Florida has a long history of labor exploitation, predating the Civil War. Early in the twentieth century, ugly hearings and a sensational trial drew national coverage to rural North Florida, aiming scrutiny on the state's brutal convict-leasing system.

Its martyr was Martin Tabert, who was busted for vagrancy in 1922 and turned over to a work camp, where a "whipping boss" beat him to death.

Clifford Tabert, who was eighty-seven in 2004, said at the time that he didn't remember much about his uncle. But he clearly recalled another man who came by his North Dakota family home about 1932; Clifford was then about fifteen.

"He was in that camp," Clifford Tabert said in an interview in January 2001. "He took off his shirt and it was all like beefsteak. Red and black and blue. I saw it."

The family has only one photograph remaining of Martin Tabert, the farm boy who never returned to Munich, North Dakota.

"He wanted to see the world," Clifford Tabert said. "He saw the bad part of it, I guess."

North Dakota farm boy Martin Tabert was busted for vagrancy and turned over to a North Florida work camp, where a "whipping boss" beat him to death. *Tabert family.*

Martin Tabert died over eighty cents, the estimated train fare he stole by jumping aboard without a ticket near Tallahassee in January 1922.

Tabert, just twenty-two, left his 560-acre farm to see the world. But when he ran out of money and couldn't pay a twenty-five-dollar vagrancy fine, he was sentenced to ninety days. He was leased out for twenty-five dollars to help lay a railroad bed for the Putnam Lumber Co.

Florida, made destitute by its role as the Confederacy's breadbasket late in the Civil War, found that it could make money, and replace the slave force, by leasing out convicts. One 1886 report said that states made a profit of nearly 400 percent over the cost of maintaining prisons. The practice was outlawed in 1905 at the state level—but not in the counties.

Why the county system was not done away with at the same time "only certain employers of labor on a large scale and conniving politicians could explain," the *New York Times* editorialized in April 1923.

Tabert, en route to the labor camp, wired home, saying, "In trouble and need 50 dollars to pay fine for vagrancy." His family wired seventy-five dollars to Tallahassee; it arrived six days after his arrest. But the sheriff returned it unopened. The Taberts presumed that their son had found a way out of his jam and had moved on.

Putnam Lumber then wrote to the Taberts that their son had died of a fever and complications and had been buried in a grave that has never been found.

To the Taberts, something stunk.

In July 1922, Glen Thompson, who had been one of Martin's bunkmates, tracked down Martin's parents and gave them the truth.

Thompson told them that he had seen their son repeatedly tortured in the camp and finally given more than one hundred lashes. Remarkably, the young man was then told to return to work. But within days, he was dead.

North Dakota legislators called on their Florida counterparts to investigate the death. Governor Cary Hardee promised to look into the case but sniffed that no state treated its convicts more humanely than did Florida.

The Talbert family filed a $50,000 lawsuit against Putnam and wrote to the nation's ten largest newspapers. A *New York World* reporter began writing daily dispatches from Florida; they would win the paper a Pulitzer Prize.

Pressured legislators finally formed a joint committee to look into convict leasing. More than one hundred witnesses told horror stories of beatings. Another camp reported no fewer than nine deaths; none of them was ever investigated.

An easy target for scrutiny was Walter Higginbotham, Putnam's "whipping boss." He later admitted to flogging up to ten prisoners a week.

His tool of choice: a "Black Aunty," a five-foot-long, seven-and-a-half-pound rawhide strap.

One inmate said that Higginbotham would drag his strap through sugar and sand between each blow. Another convict said he was beaten so severely that he could not lie on his back for a month. Yet another said that men worked waist deep in swamp water.

Guard A.P. Shivers testified that conditions had taken their toll on Tabert and that on the day he was beaten, he could not keep up on a two-mile march.

Higginbotham "gave him about 30 licks as Tabert groaned and screamed for mercy," Shivers recounted. "Tabert kept on twitching his body, so Higginbotham placed the heel of his boot on the youth's neck to make him keep his body rigid. He then gave him about 40 or 50 more licks."

When Tabert couldn't get up, the boss gave him another twenty-five, Shivers said.

"At first, I heard screams which grew weaker and weaker," said Mrs. Walter Lyles, who had been fishing near the camp. "Finally, there was only the sound of the lash."

Legislators discovered a cruel conspiracy: Leon County sheriff J.R. Jones and Judge B.F. Willis had a deal to funnel workers to the lumber company. Men charged with vagrancy were brought before Willis, sometimes late at night, and urged to plead guilty.

Documents showed that in the seven months before the deal was made, only 20 men were arrested for riding trains without tickets; in the ensuing seven months, 154 were arrested. Published reports said that Jones netted more than $2,500. The committee recommended that both Jones and Willis be removed from office.

Higginbotham went on trial in June 1923 in Lake City for first-degree murder. He admitted that he had whipped Tabert but denied having held Tabert's neck with his boot.

A jury later convicted Higginbotham of a lesser charge of second-degree murder, and he was sentenced to twenty years in prison.

A year later, the Florida Supreme Court ordered a new trial on a technicality. It never happened.

The lawsuit against Putnam Lumber was settled for $20,000.

Horrified by the abuses—and not a little worried about how the bad publicity would hurt the tourist trade—the state legislature outlawed convict leasing in May 1923.

Originally published in the *Palm Beach Post*, February 1, 2004.

The Ashley Gang

The bridge at San Sebastian isn't there anymore. Replaced decades ago by a newer road, only its weathered pilings protrude from the marsh grass, marking the dead. It was at this rural spot near the Indian River–Brevard County line where the Ashley gang met its ignoble end on November 1, 1924.

In 1983, Ada Coates Williams stood before a Florida Historical Society convention in Daytona Beach and settled once and for all how the gang died.

From the start, many had challenged the official police version that the gang members were shot escaping. Most people believed from the get-go that the Ashleys were assassinated by lawmen tired of being humiliated from the Stuart National Bank to the Miami jail. Williams uncovered the real story from a retired deputy who was on the bridge that night.

The former deputy admitted that the five gangsters were executed. His one condition for sharing the story was that Williams not reveal his testimony until after all of the deputies involved had died. She kept her promise; her talk came just months after the last one was gone.

At that 1983 meeting, a fellow instructor told her that she had a book in the making. No one had written a lengthy tome on the Ashleys since Hix Stuart in 1928. But Williams was as good a candidate as any. She was there.

"My father knew all these people," Williams said in 1997. "Everybody knew everybody else in those days. I was four. I remember my father being so upset that they were murdered."

Her book updates the Hix Stuart story, which glossed over the gang's slaying. Like the 1928 book, Williams's is brief, only forty-five pages with a twenty-four-page appendix of documents.

At first, Williams, a retired teacher of creative writing at Fort Pierce's Indian River Community College whose family had settled the area in the 1870s, wasn't interested.

"My life had been so entwined with these people that I kept their confidence," she said in 1997. "It's a book I didn't want to write. It's a paper I didn't want to do." But, she added, "it was the last time someone could give the story, documented."

If he were alive today, John Ashley might be just another street thug. Instead, the tall man with the glass eye became South Florida's most romanticized gangster.

Long before Bonnie Parker and Clyde Barrow became America's great antiheroes, Ashley and his ragtag gang enthralled and infuriated boom-era Florida with their robbing, hijacking, rumrunning and even murder.

A page from the book *The Notorious Ashley Gang* by Hix Stuart. Palm Beach Post *archives*.

Ashley even had a "Bonnie" of his own: Laura Upthegrove, "Queen of the Everglades." And like Bonnie and Clyde, Ashley and three of his cronies ended up dead in an explosion of gunfire.

DeSoto Tiger

In 1904, Joe Ashley brought his wife and five sons from Florida's gulf coast to the tiny Broward County farm community of Pompano Beach. The Ashleys were like many hardscrabble families that farmed, hunted and did odd jobs in frontier South Florida. Joe got a job as a wood scrapper for the railroad.

A father-in-law of one of the brothers later said of young John, born in 1888, "I never saw a more mannerly or nicer boy in my life. He always came in with a smile and a pleasant word for all."

The family moved in 1911 to West Palm Beach, and John, who had become an expert trapper, spent most of his time in the Everglades, which then stretched to the south shore of Lake Okeechobee.

John Ashley, from the book *The Notorious Ashley Gang* by Hix Stuart. *Palm Beach Post archives.*

The family later moved to Gomez, near Stuart, then in Palm Beach County (Martin would split off in 1925).

Friends said that Ashley was a crack shot. He would have someone place a bottle on its side on a fence post and shoot through the mouth, blowing out the bottom but leaving the mouth intact. He could behead a quail with a single shot from forty feet away while riding a wagon.

And there was talk that the family did some moonshining out in the woods. Later, with Prohibition in 1920, the family got into the smuggling business as well, running rum to Florida from the British-held Bahamas.

Others told stories of acts of kindness by the Ashley family: leaving money or food for needy people; ditching a bank robbery after learning that the president had been a childhood playmate; and disarming but sparing a man sent to kill them, instead sending him off with a five-dollar bill.

On December 29, 1911, a dredge digging the North New River Canal from Fort Lauderdale to Lake Okeechobee uncovered the body of Seminole hunter and trader DeSoto Tiger, son of Tommy Tiger, head of the Cow Creek Seminoles.

A hunting companion told authorities that the last person seen with DeSoto Tiger was John Ashley. The Ashleys often camped and trapped with the Seminoles.

Ashley had been arrested the previous night in West Palm Beach for a reckless display of firearms; he had paid the twenty-five-dollar fine and left. Now, Palm Beach County sheriff George Baker sent two deputies to Gomez to look for Ashley. As the two walked along Dixie Highway near Hobe Sound, John Ashley and his young brother Bob leaped from the bushes, their pistols drawn.

They disarmed the lawmen and told them, "Tell Baker not to send any more chicken-hearted men with rifles or they are apt to get hurt."

The slap at Baker was the first volley in what would become a twelve-year, multigenerational verbal and blood feud between the Ashleys and the Bakers.

A two-year search—Carl Fisher, the mogul who later put Miami Beach on the map, offered a $500 reward—was fruitless. John Ashley was reported to have worked on a New Orleans boat and then at a Seattle logging camp. He finally turned himself in to Palm Beach County authorities in 1914.

Trial and Escape

In court, Ashley admitted to shooting DeSoto Tiger but said that the Seminole had threatened to shoot him if he didn't give him some liquor. Ashley was

Palm Beach County sheriff Bob Baker was instrumental in bringing the Ashley gang to justice. *Florida Photographic Collection.*

confident that the state would have a tough time convicting a white man of an Indian's murder with a minimum of evidence and no witnesses.

The case ended in a hung jury, with a nine-to-three vote to acquit.

The state had the retrial moved to Dade County, which then stretched to Deerfield Beach (Broward would be split off in 1915). Ashley didn't relish the thought of standing trial in Miami, far from friends and supporters.

Sheriff Baker's son Robert, a deputy, was charged with taking Ashley back to his Palm Beach County Jail cell; because of Ashley's good behavior, Baker didn't cuff him. Suddenly, Ashley bolted and vaulted over a ten-foot fence.

In early February 1915, the Ashleys tried to rob the Florida East Coast Railway's Palm Beach Limited, but a woman's screams alerted a porter, who locked down car doors at each end, keeping the robbers out. They fled when the train stopped a mile south of Stuart.

Sheriff Baker picked up Ashley's nephew, Hanford Mobley, along with Ashley's father and a man who worked for the family.

Then, on February 23, 1915, Ashley—along with his brother Bob and an associate, Kid Lowe—robbed the Stuart Bank of $4,300 and forced a customer to drive them away in a car that they hijacked from the front of the bank.

As they fled, they fired guns to show that they were serious gangsters.

Kid Lowe fired a gun that shattered John Ashley's jaw with the bullet resting against his left eye. Hix Stuart's 1924 book says that Lowe was shooting at pursuing policemen and the bullet struck the window frame; Williams says that Lowe deliberately shot Ashley in frustration and anger over the meager take.

Bruised and in disarray, the gang scattered into the woods, where Sheriff Baker was able to catch up with John Ashley. Lowe and Bob Ashley got away.

Newspaper accounts of the robbery referred for the first time to "the Ashley gang." Some reveled in their daring exploits; others condemned them as thieving thugs.

Ashley refused surgery to remove the bullet lodged in his head, saying that there wasn't much point if he was to be hanged for killing DeSoto Tiger. The eye was later removed, and he was fitted with a glass one.

The courts went through 150 potential jurors before giving up and moving the trial to Miami. The Dade County sheriff ordered extra locks and chains for Ashley, saying that he didn't trust the gangster to stay put. He was proven right.

Shootout at Dade County Jail

"Ashley Confident He Will Be Freed," the *Tropical Sun* reported on March 22, 1915. In court, Ashley "did not seem the least nervous or worried and watched the proceedings of the court with as much interest as one of the disinterested spectators," the *Sun* continued.

Ashley's trial was brief; it ended on April 6 in a conviction and a sentence of death.

On June 2, 1915, as the sheriff headed to lunch, he saw a young man approach the Dade County Jail on a bicycle. He figured that the visitor was some boy who wanted to talk to prisoners. He would later identify the bicyclist as Bob Ashley.

Just after 1:00 p.m., Deputy Sheriff Wilber Hendrickson answered a knock on the door of his home, adjacent to the jail.

"Are you Hendrickson?" the man asked, according to witnesses. Before Hendrickson could answer, he was struck by a rifle shot.

Bob Ashley took the keys from the dying Hendrickson and started for the jail. But the commotion alerted Hendrickson's wife, who tried to stop Bob. The man panicked. He turned heel, dropped the keys and jumped into a passing car.

The driver, T.R. Durkett, told the *Miami Metropolis* that Ashley placed a gun to his head and ordered him to drive away "or I will blow your head off."

After a few blocks, Bob Ashley took the wheel, but two police officers caught up with him a few blocks from the jail. Officer John Reinhart Riblet told Bob that he was under arrest. Bob fired; so did the officer. Both were mortally wounded. Two other officers pounced on Bob.

Riblet was the first Miami police officer to be killed in the line of duty.

Dade County sheriff Dan Hardie went to John Ashley's cell and asked if the man who had shot the jailer was his brother and if he had known of the jailbreak attempt. Ashley said no, twice.

Ashley would try another breakout. For five weeks, he dug a hole in his cell floor with a spoon. But jailers found the hole while he showered. They waited until he was two feet from escape before letting on to him.

On August 11, 1916, the Florida Supreme Court threw out the murder charges. Ashley was returned to Palm Beach County, where he was convicted in the Stuart bank robbery and sentenced to seventeen and a half years at the Florida State Prison in Raiford. He arrived on November 23.

On March 31, 1918, he was assigned to a road camp. Three months later, he escaped, along with another bank robber, Tom Maddox, and fled to the Everglades.

Waiting there was Laura Upthegrove.

Queen of the Everglades

The woman identified as John Ashley's girlfriend was part of the Upthegrove family that had settled along the northeast shore of Lake Okeechobee; Upthegrove Beach, north of Port Mayaca, is named for them.

One report described her as "a large woman with dark hair, a deep suntan, and wore a .38 caliber revolver strapped to her waist." She allegedly helped plan robberies and shipments of rum. She was dubbed "Queen of the Everglades."

Ashley was on the lam for three years; in that time, he reportedly ran three Palm Beach County stills and joined brothers Ed and Frank to run rum from West End, on Grand Bahama Island, only sixty miles off the Florida coast.

In June 1921, while John Ashley made a delivery at Wauchula, the local sheriff nabbed him. He didn't realize who he had until a cellmate fingered Ashley.

The gangster was returned to Raiford.

One night in October 1921, John Ashley, asleep in his cell bunk, had a dream. Brothers Ed and Frank Ashley were in a boat on the open ocean; a storm rocked the vessel. Suddenly, three other smugglers jumped the boat and killed the two brothers.

Ashley contacted his father and learned that Frank and Ed had left Bimini on October 21 in rough weather and never returned.

Ashley escaped once more.

In November 1923, Joe Tracey hailed a cab in Pompano. He had the driver take him into the woods, where the rest of the gang leaped out, tied him to a tree and drove his taxi into town. As John Ashley left, he told the cabbie where he could find his car later and gave the man a bullet. "Tell Baker we'll be waiting for him in the Everglades," Ashley told the driver.

The Pompano Bank was a rich target. The gang made off with $5,000 in cash and $18,000 in securities. Ashley gave the cashier a bullet, calling it a souvenir.

Baker, meanwhile, had received that bullet left with the cabbie, and in February 1924, he went after the Ashleys. He gathered a posse and several deputies, including Fred Baker, who wasn't related.

At dawn, they opened fire at the Ashley camp in western Martin County. Joe Ashley was struck down as he tied his shoes. John, seeing his father hit, killed Fred Baker. The gang then fled into the woods.

Angry townspeople burned the camp and then went to the Ashley and Mobley homes and burned them as well.

In September 1924, a woman in a white blouse, a long black skirt and a hat entered the Stuart Bank. It was really Hanford Mobley in disguise. Middleton and Matthews waited in the getaway car. The Ashley gang was hitting the same bank it had struck before.

The robbers fled in a car they had stolen from a man in Gomez whom they had tied to a tree.

Their pursuer this time wasn't George Baker. It was his son, Bob, that young jailer John Ashley had tricked when he fled the Palm Beach County Jail in 1914. Bob was now the sheriff.

First Mobley and Middleton were nabbed in Plant City, near Tampa, and then Matthews in Griffin, Georgia.

After several failed escape attempts, Mobley was moved to the Broward County Jail in Fort Lauderdale. Sure enough, he broke out, along with Matthews.

Middleton refused to go; he was later transferred to Raiford, where he met two new cronies, Ray Lynn and Joe Tracey, who had earlier joined forces with John Ashley during his time in prison.

Joe Tracey finished his term at Raiford, and Lynn and Middleton escaped a Panhandle road camp. Mobley, who had driven a cab in

California and worked a liner to Germany, also returned. The gang was whole again.

The Ashleys continued their rumrunning, hijacking, thefts and robberies and earned a new enemy: St. Lucie sheriff J.R. Merritt.

Bob Baker had not forgotten them, either. Nor had Ashley forgotten Bob. He frequently sent him bullets, saying that he still had one with Baker's name on it. One day, Baker shot back, "I'll wear your glass eye on my watch fob."

The Ashleys, meanwhile, had learned that some of the rum they had bought on a recent run to Bimini was water. Eluding deputies through the Jupiter Inlet, they raided four wholesale houses of $8,000 in money and liquor. Later, it was learned that $225,000 had been sent that morning to a bank in Nassau.

Baker heard that the Ashleys planned to head to Jacksonville, lay low until after an upcoming election and then return to kill the sheriff before fleeing Florida.

Author Ada Williams contends that the tip came from none other than Laura Upthegrove, affronted when Ashley opted to flee without her.

Baker alerted Merritt, his St. Lucie counterpart, that Ashley might be heading his way. He sent up deputies Elmer Padgett, Henry Stubbs, L.B. Thomas and O.B. Padgett, telling them to chase the Ashleys to Georgia if they had to.

The Palm Beach County lawmen joined Merritt and two of his men at a spot just north of Sebastian and about twenty-eight miles north of Fort Pierce: the bridge at St. Sebastian River.

The Lantern on the Bridge

At about 10:45 p.m. on a Saturday, the night after Halloween 1924, a red lantern swung lazily back and forth on a chain strung across a wooden bridge that spanned the St. Sebastian River, near the St. Lucie–Brevard county line (Indian River County was formed in 1925).

Two youngsters from Sebastian pulled up the bridge. The sheriff stepped from the bushes and told them to drive on.

Behind them, the Ford bearing Ashley, Lynn, Middleton and Mobley came to a stop.

The lawmen poured from the bushes and surrounded the car. The two young men had turned around to return to Sebastian, and their headlights fell on four men standing handcuffed on the bridge. They raced to town to tell everyone that the Ashleys had been captured.

Before they got there, the four Ashley gang members were dead.

Ashley still held his rifle and wore two pistols as well. Weapons were also found near the other three dead men. In the car was found a large supply of ammunition, along with some food—baked ham, beans, potatoes— and clothing.

The bodies were taken to Fort Pierce, where they were displayed on the grass in front of a mortuary. In the morning, they were laid out on a sidewalk in front of the funeral home. Townspeople gawked at the fallen gangsters.

A judge called a coroner's inquest.

The official story was that Ashley and his gang had raised their hands to deputies on the bridge, but when Ashley saw the glint of the red lantern on the handcuffs, his phobia of the manacles caused him to drop his hands and shout, "Shoot boys. They'll never put those things on me." Almost instantly the deputies opened fire.

But already word was spreading that the Ashleys had been executed.

A young lawyer, Alto Adams, represented the Ashley family. They claimed that their son and his friends had intended to go straight and were murdered by the law.

Adams called for the bodies to be examined for handcuff marks on the wrists. It never happened.

A grove worker who also worked part time at the mortuary told his boss that he saw the bodies brought in, stacked in the patrol car, with their hands still cuffed; he said that the cuffs were removed before the bodies were displayed. The worker was never called to testify. The undertaker said he saw no marks.

The two Sebastian men who had been on the bridge told what they had seen. A lawyer for the deputies cross-examined them for hours; they stuck to their stories.

The judge ruled the shootings justifiable. The deputies took an oath never to speak again of that night on the bridge.

John Ashley, Hanford Mobley and Ray Lynn were buried at the Ashley plot in Gomez. At Laura Upthegrove's request, representatives of the Salvation Army conducted services. Leugenia Ashley wept for her husband and four sons, all victims of violence.

In February 1929, Baker, the Palm Beach County sheriff, received a crudely written letter postmarked days earlier in Shreveport, Louisiana. The anonymous writer signed the note, "Your Future Murderer." He said that he had assembled a gang of eleven men in New Orleans, "and our first job will be to bump you off."

The writer said that his group included the two Ashley brothers who had disappeared at sea during their liquor run from the Bahamas. Baker believed that the note was the ramblings of an Ashley groupie, and he didn't plan to lose any sleep over it.

Baker's would-be stalker couldn't have been Heywood Register. Baker and two deputies, F.H. Packwood and Sebastian Bridge veteran Elmer Padgett, had gunned down the minor Ashley gang member the previous month in a shootout in Boynton Beach.

Following the Ashleys' deaths, St. Lucie County sheriff J.R. Merritt received numerous telegrams, some of which were published in the Hix Stuart book. Many of the originals were kept by his grandson, Fort Pierce real estate agent Edwin "Hap" Merritt, who also has the Winchester rifle J.R. took from John Ashley the night the gang was killed.

"The Ashley gang were murderers, bank robbers, and smugglers with a long history of jailbreaks and killing law enforcement officers," Hap told private eye and retired New York police detective Warren J. Sonne for an October 2007 article in *Indian River Magazine*. "No way my granddad was going to put them in the little Fort Pierce jail."

Three days after the slayings on the bridge, Sheriff Merritt was reelected.

The rumors of an execution of the Ashleys continued to dog the sheriff, and he was voted out of office two years later. The controversy pursued him through years as a county commissioner, as well as his family and those of the deputies.

In a 1969 *Miami Herald* article, the two men who, as youngsters, had been on the bridge—and who were now in their sixties—told the story of what they had seen.

The deputy already had confided to Ada Williams. He said that the deputies, convinced that no jail could hold the gang members, had determined to finish them.

Williams wrote that her confidant had cuffed John Ashley and told him not to move and to keep his hands over his head while colleagues cuffed the other gangsters. She wrote that Sheriff Merritt had been at the end of the bridge and had not given the order to open fire.

"Suddenly John Ashley took a quick step forward and started to drop his handcuffed hands, and the deputy guarding him fired," Williams wrote. "He said that he supposed the other prisoners tried to break, or that the deputies feared that John had fired on him, for suddenly there was a lot of shooting, and they were all killed." According to Williams, the deputy never apologized for the act, saying that Ashley had promised to kill lawmen if given a chance.

"It was them or us at that point," the deputy told her.

The retired deputy said that he scooped out Ashley's glass eye for Sheriff Baker, but it was later returned to the family for burial. The deputy said had he known that would happen he would have ground the eye beneath his heel.

The greatest crime involving the Ashley gang might have been the 1970s cinematic vandalism called *Little Laura and Big John*. It was filmed in 1971 in Stuart, and locals had high hopes that it would bring the world the sensational tale of the gang.

Instead, the world got an "incoherent, amateurish muddle of a flick," according to a 2002 article in the *Fort Pierce Tribune*. "Starring cross-eyed wax-work actors Karen Black (pre–*Five Easy Pieces* and *Nashville*) and Frankie Avalon wannabe Fabian Forte as the title moll and mobster, the no-budget crime noir will never be mistaken for *Bonnie and Clyde*, its obvious role model."

The last surviving member of the gang, Joe Tracy, was in and out of prison most of his life, and he died in prison in Raiford in September 1968. He was eighty-two.

Not long after the Ashleys were buried in 1924, Laura Upthegrove died as well. At a small store she ran in Canal Point, she got into an argument with a customer over change, grabbed a bottle of cleaning fluid from a shelf and drank it, falling dead in minutes.

Valda Padgett, Laura's sister, lived into her nineties in Vero Beach but refused—unless she was paid for it—to speak on the record, except to say that virtually everything written about her sister was a lie. Nor would she provide a copy of the photograph she still had of a young Laura, frozen in youth.

The Ashleys: A Chronology

March 19, 1888: John Ashley is born near Fort Myers.

1911: The Ashleys move to West Palm Beach and then to Gomez, near Hobe Sound.

December 29, 1911: John Ashley murders DeSoto Tiger, the son of Tommy Tiger, head of the Cow Creek Seminoles. Tiger's body is found in a canal northwest of Fort Lauderdale. Ashley surrenders two years later but escapes after the jury in the murder trial deadlocks.

February 1915: Ashley, his father and his nephew, Hanford Mobley, try to rob a Florida East Coast Railway train, but a woman's screams stop them, and the gang flees one mile south of Stuart.

February 23, 1915: John, his brother Bob and Kid Lowe rob the Stuart Bank. Lowe fires a shot that shatters John Ashley's jaw and rests against his left eye. Sheriff Baker catches only John Ashley, who refuses surgery to remove the bullet. He is later fitted with a glass eye.

June 2, 1915: Trying to spring John Ashley from jail, brother Bob kills, and is killed by, a Miami police officer.

Summer 1918: Ashley escapes from road camp and spends three years operating stills in northern Palm Beach County and running rum from the Bahamas.

October 1921: John's brothers Ed and Frank disappear while returning from the Bahamas with rum.

November 1923: Ashley and his gang steal a cab and rob the Pompano Bank. Ashley leaves the cabbie a bullet and dares Palm Beach County sheriff Bob Baker, George Baker's son, to look for him in the Everglades.

February 1924: Sheriff Baker's posse opens fire at the Ashley camp in western Martin County. Joe Ashley, John's father, is shot as he ties his shoes. John, seeing his father hit, kills deputy Fred Baker.

September 1924: John Ashley's nineteen-year-old slender nephew, Hanford Mobley, dresses in a white blouse, a long black skirt, a hat and a veil. "She" robs the Stuart Bank.

October 1924: Gang member Joe Tracey, who had left the gang, is captured in Kissimmee on an FEC Railroad branch line train.

November 1, 1924: The shootout at the St. Sebastian Bridge.

The Ashley Gang

Outlaws of the Everglades: Big John and Little Laura
John Ashley (1888–1924), leader of the Ashley gang
Laura Upthegrove (1897[?]–1927), "Queen of the Everglades" and John Ashley's girlfriend

The Ashley Family
Joe Ashley (1861–1924), John's father
Leugenia Ashley (1862–1946), John's mother
Bob Ashley (1894–1915), John's brother; killed in attempt to spring John from Dade County Jail
Ed (1880–1921) and Frank (1900–1921) Ashley, John's brothers; never returned from a rum smuggling run to the Bahamas
Bill Ashley (1883–1940), the only Ashley brother who survived the family business; he settled in Pompano Beach

Killed on the St. Sebastian Bridge
John Ashley
Hanford Mobley, Ashley's nephew
Ray "Shorty" Lynn, from an old Florida family; he married young and joined the army but fled the military and his pregnant wife and eventually joined the gang
John Clarence Middleton, reputedly a dope addict who moved from Chicago

Other Gang Members
Tom Maddox, known bank robber; joined with Ashley in prison and fled with him in 1918
Kid Lowe, seasoned bank robber who moved from Chicago; shot Ashley—accidentally or otherwise—during a botched robbery of Pompano Bank in 1915
Albert Miller, arrested during a 1924 raid on an Ashley camp
Joe Tracey, recaptured after a 1924 escape from a Marianna road gang
Ray Young Matthews, took turns with Middleton leading the gang during Ashley's jail times; he was never recaptured after his 1924 escape from Broward Jail
Heywood Register, minor gang member killed by deputies in January 1929 in a shootout in Boynton Beach

The Rest of the Story

THE PADGETTS

Was O.B. Padgett one of the deputies who "captured" the Ashley gang?
—D.S. Padgett, Lamont, Florida

Mr. Padgett, the inquirer, doesn't say whether he is related to the deputy who was part of one of the most dramatic moments in the history of Treasure Coast crime.

On November 1, 1924, deputies stopped John Ashley and colleagues Hanford Mobley, Ray "Shorty" Lynn and John Middleton on a wooden bridge over the St. Sebastian River in what was then St. Lucie County. Deputies said that the gang members were shot because they tried to escape. But many believed that the Ashleys were assassinated.

As early as 1928, Hix Stuart's *The Notorious Ashley Gang* identified O.B. Padgett as one of the four Palm Beach County deputies, along with two St. Lucie deputies and the sheriff, who were on the bridge.

In 1997, Ada Coats Williams, a retired teacher of creative writing at Fort Pierce's Indian River Community College, completed *Florida's Ashley Gang*, the first book on the Ashleys since 1928. A retired deputy who had been on the bridge that night had, in the 1950s, confirmed to her that the men were shot while handcuffed, after John made a sudden move. He offered this information on the condition that she keep the secret until after all those involved had died.

Ten years later, in October 2007, in *Indian River Magazine*, Warren J. Sonne, a private eye and a retired New York police detective, revealed the deputy he was convinced had shot Ashley and confided to Ada Williams.

Sonne interviewed Ed Register, a ninety-year-old retired chamber of commerce executive who, as a seven-year-old, had seen the bodies laid out in front of a Fort Pierce mortuary.

"No, no handcuffs in sight," Register recalled.

He also noted that Ada Williams's 1997 book came out the same year that retired deputy O.E. "Three-Fingers" Wiggins, the last survivor of the deputies on the bridge, died in a Bartow nursing home.

But Sonne concludes that Williams's "Deep Throat" was Elmer Padgett.

Padgett, who died at age fifty-six in 1964, was one of the deputies who took part in the raid on the Ashley still that left Joe Ashley dead. Williams lists a 1958 interview with him.

Articles on the Ashley gang in the summer of 2008 prompted Alice L. Luckhardt of Stuart to write us a note. Here are excerpts:

> *In your recent reply in the* **PB** *Post of June 17th and June 18th about O.B. Padgett, former chief of police of Stuart and a posse member in the capture of the Ashley Gang of 1924, I have some additional information for you.*

First, the individual who requested the information, "D.S. Padgett," is Donna S. Padgett, wife of James "Jim" Padgett, only son of O.B. Padgett. She had placed that query some time ago.

Over the last couple of years I have corresponded with Jim Padgett and other Padgett relatives for research I was doing on the life and times of O.B. Padgett. Jim was of great help providing various documents but did not fully know the events, especially surrounding the Ashley Gang.

He did have some typed recollections his father had done in the mid-1970s, which he sent me. Unfortunately several key pages were missing. By contacting some of the other Padgett relatives (nephews), it turned out I was able to piece together the complete 27 pages of O.B.'s typed unpublished recollections of his days in Stuart and especially about the Ashley Gang.

Second, for the Stuart Heritage (president, Chris Sawicki), I spoke at Stuart City Hall on June 10th. As a complete surprise to me, present in the audience was Jim and Donna Padgett, who had come down from Taylor County for the presentation.

Third, I have produced a book, O.B. Padgett—A Florida Son *(Lulu Publishing).*

Luckhardt's website is www.Lulu.com/content.

JOHN ASHLEY'S RIFLE

On June 16, 2008, William M. Barnes walked into the old Palm Beach County Courthouse to donate a piece of South Florida history. It almost got him arrested.

"Just a quiet little visit to the place I worked at," Barnes, who died in February 2009, said with a laugh at the time. "Turned out to be quite an event. I'm glad to see they're so on their toes."

Barnes, then eighty-seven, West Palm Beach's police chief for two decades, had decided to find a permanent home for a rifle he had received in the 1940s or 1950s from the nephew of Palm Beach County sheriff Bob Baker, who was the nemesis of legendary gangster John Ashley.

The rifle was one of two found in Ashley's car on the night of November 1, 1924, on a bridge near Sebastian, when deputies ambushed him and three colleagues.

"I didn't want anything to happen to it," said Barnes, who retired as police chief in 1980 but also had a brief stint as acting chief in 1985. "I didn't want anybody selling it on eBay."

So, as he prepared to head to his Georgia summer home, he contacted a curator at the Historical Society of Palm Beach County, which is housed at the recently restored courthouse and operates the Richard and Pat Johnson Palm Beach County History Museum.

"He said, yes, they would love to have it," Barnes said. "They told me to come on down."

About 1:30 p.m., Barnes drove from his home near Forest Hill Boulevard and Federal Highway to the museum and parked at the adjacent garage. Then he calmly entered through a side door, carrying a rifle.

"I never gave it a thought," he said.

"He shows up with the thing over his shoulder like it's something casual," society president and chief executive Loren Mintz recalled. "He says, 'I want to go to the museum.' But he's got this rifle. She (the receptionist) says, 'Just a minute. I want to make this call.' Of course, she called the sheriff."

Deputies who handle security across North Dixie Highway at the new courthouse came running.

"We had a call that a man walked into the old courthouse with what appeared to be a rifle." Sergeant Teresa Bloeser said. "He just unfortunately carried it in and freaked out everybody."

Deputies "just kept coming," Barnes said. "They were polite and everything, but they wouldn't listen to me. I understood they were just doing their job."

Barnes said none drew weapons. He told them that the gun was not loaded, and a society official confirmed Barnes's story.

The society said it would display the rifle with a previously donated Ashley shotgun. "It's a wonderful addition," Mintz said.

Expanded from articles originally published in the *Palm Beach Post*, March 13, 1997; December 6, 2000; November 7, 2007; June 17, 2008; June 18, 2008; August 6, 2008; and February 9, 2009.

Hypocrite's Row

Prohibition in Florida

"Florida Is as Dry as the Sahara Desert"

Palm Beach was dry but hardly sober.

If you wanted to drink at the Royal Poinciana Hotel, you had to sneak down a hallway dubbed "Hypocrite's Row." And at the Breakers, you could drink till you dropped—if you dropped discreetly. In Palm Beach, as elsewhere in South Florida, Prohibition barely put a dent in the partying.

Booze was no stranger to the New World. On Christopher Columbus's second voyage, in 1493, he brought sugar cane from the Canary Islands and planted it on Hispaniola. His aim was to feed Europe's sweet tooth.

But soon Europeans in the Caribbean learned that if they crushed the cane, cooked its juice into molasses and fermented that with yeast, they created a magical substance that brought its users and merchants either to heaven or hell. They called it "rumbullion," from an English slang term for "uproar," and later shortened that to rum.

By the early 1900s, decent people declared—publicly, if not privately—that rum and its cousins were America's ruination.

Enter Prohibition. The noble experiment went into effect on January 16, 1920, and lasted until 1933. But it never took hold in the wide-open boom

The Mediterranean ballroom at the Breakers Hotel, Palm Beach, about 1925. The ballroom, measuring 52 by 118 feet, was used only three times a year, for dancing during the social season. *The Breakers*.

towns of South Florida, which had already been ignoring local temperance laws for decades.

Here was a thirsty tourist trade, with local officials vulnerable to corruption, miles of open beaches and coves, a vast Everglades to hide stills and a smuggling pipeline from the nearby islands.

"I would be a little careful in bringing back much liquor," an associate wrote to famed Miami Beach developer Carl Fisher from Indiana in April 1923. "I got through with two cases O.K. in trunks and suit cases but the enforcement officers are very active all over the state. They have recently sent ten of our bootlegging citizens to the penitentiary, out of this county alone."

Mostly, what Prohibition did was turn South Florida's lucrative alcohol business over to criminals. Mobsters oversaw stills, smuggling and distribution to hotels and speakeasies and ran many establishments themselves.

Bahamians also cashed in big. Shipments from England totaled 80,000 gallons in 1918, 500,000 gallons five years later and 1.5 million gallons in 1930. A case of liquor was $18 in the Bahamas, double that in South Florida and as much as $100 up North.

Boats would shuttle the liquor from Nassau to West End and Bimini, less than sixty miles from Florida. Contraband was then packed in "hams," six bottles to a burlap sack, padded with paper and straw.

Rumrunning became routine.

Beth Spencer once lived in a house designed for rumrunning. "It was on 38th Street in West Palm Beach. The basement opened to the water, so the rumrunners would come right in," she said in 1995 from Riviera Beach.

To the south on Olive Avenue was Zada Rogerson's family home, built in 1924. Rogerson remembered her father helping dig trenches at night to bury rum alongside the houses.

At the Breakers, a private dining room was built for those who wanted a drink with dinner. "You couldn't serve liquor in a public dining room— Prohibition was such a hot social issue," Breakers historian Jim Ponce said. "If the people next to you happened to be Prohibitionists, God knows what would happen."

Some lawmen did their best to stop the flow of booze.

In a September 1922 report to the federal Prohibition agency, Palm Beach County sheriff Bob Baker listed forty-six stills destroyed; 95 gallons of moonshine, 232 barrels of mash and 232 gallons of other liquor seized; and forty-one people arrested, with twenty-two of them convicted.

Other lawmen were perhaps less committed. In 1920, State Attorney Thompson convinced a judge in an Okeechobee bootlegger's case that

Thompson should hold the contraband for safekeeping. He and a deputy loaded it in his Model T and set out for West Palm Beach.

When the grand jury next met, the evidence had disappeared.

A few days later, Governor Sidney J. Catts suspended Thompson for "public drunkenness and neglect of official duties." Remarkably, Thompson was reelected, and the governor, opting for discretion, restored him to office.

None of it mattered.

Even Florida's lawmakers had trouble getting respect when it came to the state's hedonistic image. Once, during a U.S. House debate on Prohibition, a representative from Florida insisted, "Florida is as dry as the Sahara desert."

He was drowned out by laughter and promptly sat down.

Expanded from articles originally published in the *Palm Beach Post*, January 23, 1995, and October 16, 2002.

A 1923 image of Edgar Thompson, scandal-plagued Palm Beach County prosecutor. *Historical Society of Palm Beach County*.

The Gulf Stream Pirate

It was too quiet. From the deck of his own vessel, Beckwith Jordan looked through the mid-afternoon glare and saw Coast Guard Patrol Boat 249 rocking on the waves of the open ocean. A thirty-footer that could only be a rumrunner was tied to its stern, and a distress flag flapped from the 249's mast.

All three boats were some thirty-five miles from Fort Lauderdale and Coast Guard Base 6, and the two boats Jordan was nearing rolled with the swells. Not a sound rose above the lapping of water.

Jordan, head of Base 6, had been pulled from the ball field by a radio report from the 249, saying that it had captured some rumrunners and they were "giving some trouble" and trying to set the patrol boat on fire. The commander's boat had raced some thirty-five miles in fifty minutes.

Beckwith ordered his crew to move alongside the 249 and its catch. As he drew closer to the two boats, his eyes grew wider and his throat tighter.

Blood mixed with salt water slid up and down the seventy-five feet of deck boards on the rocking 249. The grim rivulets routed around immovable obstacles: gunwales and bulkheads and bodies. The bodies of Jordan's crew. His colleagues. His friends.

Skipper Sidney Cantwell Sanderlin was already dead. Blood and gore from his chest soaked the pilothouse. Secret Service agent Bob Webster was also dead, his abdomen torn by slugs.

James Horace Alderman, the "Gulf Stream Pirate." *Fort Lauderdale Historical Society.*

Coast Guard cook Jodie Hollingsworth and chief engineer Victor Lamby lay moaning and bleeding. Slugs had torn away Hollingsworth's right eye and much of his face, but he would live. A bullet had ripped into Lamby's back and stopped near his spine; four days later he would become the third fatality.

Four other guardsmen stood unhurt but stunned into silence.

Around the mount that held the boat's one-pound gun, two men, bruised and bloody, were trussed up like rodeo calves, tied with handcuffs and rope lines.

Robert Weech was alert. James Horace Alderman was half conscious. He had been stabbed a half dozen times with an ice pick, stomped in the ribs and smashed in the head with fists, a pistol butt, an oar and a scraper.

The cockpit of the rumrunner was packed with twenty "hams," each burlap sack holding six one-quart bottles.

Jordan shouted commands, and the three boats headed toward the Florida coast. Alderman's boat never made it. It caught fire under tow and sank.

At 7:00 p.m., just four hours after the shootout on the high seas, Jordan called to order an inquiry at the base. Only then did he hear the full account of the horrific battle that one Coast Guard officer would call "the most dramatic sea fight in the history of the service."

That long and bloody Sunday, August 7, 1927, was drawing to a close. The board quit just after midnight. It returned at 9:00 a.m. on Monday, and by noon, the men had heard enough.

Jordan and the board declared that James Horace Alderman and Robert E. Weech should be charged with murder and piracy on the high seas. The ensuing months would bring high drama to an upside-down region where rumrunners were Robin Hoods and federal agents thugs.

Already a champion of the wets, Alderman the prisoner found religion and a soap box, and he became an icon. Many still debate whether he was a martyr or just another common criminal.

When the "Gulf Stream Pirate" came to a Fort Lauderdale federal courtroom, it was as if the dry laws, not him, were on trial.

"I've Taken Enough of the Coast Guard"

Federal Prohibition agents—"dry men"—enforced a law that many people despised. Rumrunners and bootleggers were glorified for getting around the law and getting the people what they wanted. One such man was Alderman. He had been a fishing guide in the Fort Myers area, but soon he turned to the bigger payoffs of smuggling Chinese nationals into Florida.

Some reports suggest that, while his modern-day "jump off" counterparts drop their human cargo into the water miles offshore to avoid detection, often leading to their drownings, Alderman took money up front and then murdered clients outright.

Alderman hired a cook who turned out to be an undercover federal operative. The cook had seen enough for a warrant to be issued for Alderman in Tampa. But a friend of Alderman saw the "cook" in court and tipped the rumrunner.

Alderman bolted from southwest Florida and shifted his cargo from human to liquid.

Alderman and Weech left for Bimini on the night of August 6, 1927. Delayed by a bad engine, they didn't arrive until daybreak. Tipped that a U.S. Coast Guard ship was in harbor, they used another boat to pick up their load and then left midday on Sunday, August 7.

Hours earlier, about 9:30 a.m., Coast Guard Boat 249 had left Fort Lauderdale. Coast Guard Base 6, established in 1922, had replaced the Fort Lauderdale House of Refuge, set up in 1875 as little more than its name implied. It was a five-room house stocked with water and food, with a "sick bay" to handle survivors of shipwrecks.

Between 1922 and 1940, the base would expand the property from five acres to thirty-three. It would host sixty-five buildings, including barracks, as well as a radio room, a seaplane hangar and an armory. It boasted a fleet of six "picket boats." One was boat 249, now headed for Bimini, carrying Webster, the Secret Service agent.

Webster was checking out complaints that smugglers were dumping counterfeit U.S. currency into the Bahamian economy. In his pocket, with his Secret Service badge, American Legion pin and keys were sixteen dollars in real cash and sixteen fake fifty-dollar gold certificates.

At about 1:30 p.m., about two thirds of the way to Bimini, the crew of 249 heard the sound of a motor. Soon they spotted the boat carrying Alderman and Weech.

Ships normally didn't confront boats at sea; crewmember Hal M. Caudle recalled decades later in his memoir, *Hanging at Bahia Mar*, that Sanderlin decided to stop Alderman in order to give Webster a taste of South Florida's cops-and-robbers excitement.

When the guardsmen pulled within a half mile of the smugglers' boat, they hailed it. It didn't respond. Sanderlin pulled out his Springfield rifle and fired three rounds across its bow. The Coast Guard boat pulled alongside and tied up.

Sanderlin hopped down and asked Alderman where he was going. "Miami," the man said.

"Anything particular in the boat?"

"No."

Sanderlin pulled open a hatch and saw the hooch.

"What authority do you have to come on my boat?" Alderman demanded.

"Don't need any damned authority."

Weech piped up, telling Sanderlin that this was his first trip and he had a wife and two kids starving back in Miami. Couldn't the skipper just take the booze and let the two men go?

"Can't do that," Sanderlin said.

He ordered Alderman and Weech toward the pilothouse of the 249. He called to his crew to start unloading the contraband and radioed Base 6 for instructions.

Suddenly, Alderman turned on Sanderlin, whipped out a .45-caliber automatic and shot him in the back. Sanderlin dropped to the ground.

Chief engineer Victor Lamby reached for his own gun. Alderman rounded on him.

"I saw that he was going to shoot me so I made one jump and landed on the engine room hatch," Lamby said on his deathbed two days later. "That is when he shot me. The bullet went in my right side. That bullet was the one that cut the spinal cord."

The chief engineer fell back into the engine room hatch and did not move again.

Another guardsman, John Annis Robinson, later told investigators that as soon as he heard Alderman fire on the skipper, being unarmed, he grabbed a nearby wrench and threw it at Alderman.

"This man immediately turned around and pointed the gun at me and I dove overboard," Robinson testified.

Only seconds had passed. The men looked at one another. The only two government men who had guns wouldn't be using them. The rest of the crew's weapons lay on a chart table.

Alderman smiled.

Hours later, Coast Guardsman Lawrence Tuten told the inquiry that Sanderlin had searched Alderman for guns and found none.

"How do you think the man came in possession of this revolver?" investigators asked, referring to the .45-caliber Colt automatic, now labeled "Exhibit 1" and lying on a table in front of the tribunal.

"It must have been hidden on his person where it could not be found in a hurried search," Tuten speculated.

In 1976, Frank Lehman wrote to the Fort Lauderdale Historical Society, describing himself and his colleagues as raw teenaged recruits doing a job few people wanted. "It is evident," he said, "that we were lax in handling this situation, or it would not have happened at all."

Guardsman John Annis Robinson, meanwhile, testified at that 1927 hearing that he had climbed back onboard the boat.

"There was a bunch of sharks around there," he said. "I thought I might as well get shot as eaten up by sharks."

Alderman ordered the guardsmen to load the liquor back on his boat and herded them to its stern.

"Can you keep your mouth shut?" Alderman asked Weech. Weech said he could.

Alderman fired once into the deck. Satisfied that the gun worked, he told the men, "Now I'm going to shoot you men and burn your boat. I've taken enough off the Coast Guard."

He turned to Weech. "Break open the gas lines and fill the bilges," he ordered.

"I told him," Tuten later told the board, "he (Alderman) had best move the rum boat away from alongside as he might burn up both boats."

Alderman told his henchman to get Lamby out of the engine room and shoot him. But the earlier bullet had paralyzed the chief engineer.

"He's got to die," Alderman said. "Burn him up in there."

Then the rumrunner turned to the others.

"Alderman said, 'You may as well say your prayers. I am going to send all you sons-of-bitches to hell,'" Hal Caudle testified at Alderman's trial.

By now, it seemed only bad luck would stop Alderman. He couldn't find matches. When he went back to his boat, the engine wouldn't start. He held his gun on the government men while Weech messed with the motor.

When Alderman looked down to see how Weech was doing, Bob Webster saw his moment. The Secret Service man, and the others, rushed Alderman. The smuggler recovered quickly and fired. Webster's chest exploded.

A bullet tore away the side of Hollingsworth's face and he fell overboard.

"I saw him shooting at Lamby over the forecastle," the wounded Hollingsworth said in a sworn statement two days later. "The rummy shot the civilian passenger first and then he shot me, and that is all I remember."

Hollingsworth recalled thirty-five years later, on August 25, 1962, in a taped interview with the Fort Lauderdale Historical Society, "I'd been kicked by a mule and hit in the head with a baseball bat, but I had never been hit that hard as that .45 did."

The time Alderman had taken to shoot those two allowed the others to grab him.

"I was facing the smoking barrel of a forty-five automatic," Hal Caudle wrote in *Hanging at Bahia Mar.* "I grabbed for the gun. Got the hand with the gun in it. The gun fired. Once. Twice. Three times and quit."

Robinson had thrown Weech overboard. One of the men smacked him repeatedly with an oar as he bobbed in the water. He was finally pulled out, as was the injured Hollingsworth, who was clinging to a rope. The shot had put out his right eye.

The men beat the two crooks without mercy, "with everything we could get our hands on," Coast Guardsman Frank Lehman told the board of inquiry.

Caudle tried to finish off Alderman. "Had a forty-five in my hand," he said, "and put it against his back. Pulled the trigger and it was empty."

Alderman would later testify at his trial, "The ice pick was left in my body. As quickly as I could come to…I felt underneath of it with my elbow. This shoulder was sore, couldn't move my arm very fast. So I worked it up and pulled it out and threw it overboard. These stabs went through my lung. I was bleeding in the lungs. Blood was pouring out of my mouth."

The survivors then dragged the two rumrunners onto their boat and tied them to the gun mount. They found that the radio was working and called for help. Then they waited while Beckwith Jordan raced to their aid.

The board of inquiry later gave all four survivors promotions.

"Beats Any Dime Novel"

Four days later, about the time Lamby died, a federal judge—worried about Alderman's friends trying to break him out—ordered Alderman and Weech transferred from Fort Lauderdale to a prison in Jacksonville "in view of the alleged threats to storm the Broward County Jail."

A police car raced the men to a docked Coast Guard ship where, guarded by some thirty lawmen, they were shackled to the deck for the voyage north.

The federal government, meanwhile, had paid Florida East Coast Railway $24.52 for two one-way fares, for an official to escort Robert Webster's body to his widow in Atlanta. The Treasury Department later collected the money from Mrs. Webster.

In September, a federal grand jury indicted Alderman, accusing him of crimes "against the peace and dignity of the United States of America." The prosecutor said that the case "beats any dime novel in color and brazen defiance of the law."

Weech, who had confessed within hours of the shooting, pleaded out and got a year and a day in a federal pen in Atlanta. Records indicate that he died in February 1970 at the age of eighty-three.

Alderman's trial was set for November and then delayed to January 1928.

The press had its usual field day. A remark by Frank Tuten led to reports that Alderman had planned to force the crew to "walk the plank," and news stories were accompanied by drawings comparing Alderman to the pirate Bluebeard.

Mr. James Horace Alderman, Esquire, would have none of it. He had undergone the same miraculous conversion as so many men facing a jury: he had come to Jesus. He had begun preaching to guards and inmates and reportedly converted several. The press picked up on this story, and the man who already was a hero to some now became a downright American idol.

When his trial commenced in South Florida, Alderman came to court dressed to the nines and holding a black leather Bible. Women dressed all in white, waving fans furiously in the stifling heat, jammed the courtroom, breathing "amen" when their hero came in.

Jurors—all men, of course—were kept under armed guard to prevent the usual bribery attempts.

Prosecutors paraded in some thirty witnesses, including the assistant attorney general of the United States. They detailed the sordid history of a man who was no swashbuckling hero, just a common thug and cop killer.

Then it was Alderman's turn. He told the jury that he was "forty-three years old and a family man." He said he was just a fisherman who made so little that he lived aboard his boat.

Yes, Alderman testified, he had bought the liquor. He said that after the encounter with the coast guardsmen, he was going to bring them to Miami, turn them over to the sheriff and give himself up. He planned to dump the booze overboard on the way.

Alderman said that the men never identified themselves and he believed them to be hijackers. The crew, essentially on a delivery run for Webster, had eschewed their uniforms for T-shirts and jeans.

"I could have shot every man that I wanted to," he told the court. "I didn't have any intentions whatever of harming a man on there. I had no ill-will or hatred towards the men on that boat."

He denied rigging the gas lines to burn up the 249.

The Coast Guard alleged that Alderman had used a gun he had hidden. Alderman said that he had grabbed a gun off of a table. He claimed that he shot in self-defense after the men told him, "Now we've got you and we are going to do to you like we did Red Shannon."

Duncan W. Shannon had been riddled by coast guardsmen in the yacht basin of a Miami Beach hotel in February 1926 as guests watched, slack jawed. Amid reports that Shannon and his men were shot with their hands up, a local grand jury had indicted five guardsmen for murder, but they were eventually cleared.

The slayings of Shannon, and two other alleged rumrunners in similar circumstances, constituted Alderman's defense. But the judge wouldn't let them be introduced. Alderman's lawyer called for a mistrial, saying that the jurors had been allowed to read local newspapers—a no-no nowadays. That failed.

In fact, the jury had spent its evenings reading every spectacular detail in pages and pages of news accounts, some of them containing hearsay and speculation.

Judge Henry D. Clayton instructed the twelve gentlemen of the jury, "You are the exclusive judges of the credibility of witnesses, and the weight to be attached."

They were out four hours. Their verdict: guilty. Their recommendation: no mercy. Clayton sentenced Alderman to hang by the neck until dead.

The pirate stewed in the Jacksonville prison for ten months while his appeal ran its course. In that time, he reportedly converted five fellow prisoners and was holding prayer meetings both in Jacksonville and after he was transferred to the Dade County Jail. People of faith rushed to his support. A female Miami pastor urged a pardon or commutation. President Calvin Coolidge refused.

"If ever a case in the history of criminal jurisprudence merited—even demanded—the death penalty, this is the case," the U.S. attorney said. "I can't conceive why, while that deck was slippery with the blood of their shipmates slain by this man, those coast guardsmen didn't mete out their own justice and save us this trouble and expense."

When the U.S. Supreme Court said that it would not hear his plea, hundreds of residents, a pastor, eleven of the twelve jurors who had convicted him and even the judge who had ordered him to the gallows begged for mercy.

But in June 1929, the Justice Department and even the White House said no.

The new president, Herbert Hoover, "let me down," Alderman said. "But God is with me still."

The Nearest Port of Call

In July, Alderman's execution was set to take place at the Broward County Jail. It was a time before Florida and other states centralized their death rows and still had counties hang their worst criminals at the courthouse steps.

Fort Lauderdale–area civic leaders did not relish the outcry if they martyred the hero at the end of a very public rope. So local prosecutors demanded that the feds hang Alderman, but they didn't want the privilege either.

Finally, U.S. District Court judge Halsted L. Ritter found an obscure passage in the maritime law books. It said that a pirate captured on the high seas was to be hanged at the nearest port of call. That was determined to be the Coast Guard station in Fort Lauderdale—the very one from which the cutter had left on its fatal patrol. Ritter issued the order on August 12.

The hanging was set for five days hence: August 17, 1929.

"It's my hanging, and I want to invite my friends to it," Alderman would say. But the public wasn't invited.

As Alderman was transferred from Dade to Broward on August 15, he smiled and bid jail officials farewell. A red rose was clipped to his tie. Alderman left behind a Bible for his family to remember him as "a Christian who had placed his future in the hands of his maker."

Tipped by cops, a *Miami Herald* photographer was waiting in Fort Lauderdale. U.S. marshals thrashed him and smashed his equipment; the local authorities promptly issued arrest warrants for the federal goons.

Judge Ritter was flummoxed by all the love flowing toward the allegedly cleansed Gulf Stream Pirate. "Why is it necessary to send flowers and pudding to him?" Ritter asked.

The night before Alderman was to go to the gallows, he wrote the *Miami Herald* an open letter:

> *When this is read I will have passed over the brink of eternity into the Great Beyond.*
>
> *I would like to state through the medium of* The Miami Herald *that I am feeling fine, physically, mentally and spiritually. With the wonderful comfort and strength that I received from Jesus Christ, I am assured that when tomorrow comes I will go with smiles of comfort on my face…*
>
> *As I sit here in my cell I can look back and see just what caused me to be where I am today. Drunkenness first starts a young man to gambling—*

and swearing grows on him—and from that step he becomes hardened in his heart in envy and hatred toward mankind. Then, as he grows up, he becomes what you would call educated to crime. Bootlegging and smuggling is the next step. And there are other angles of downfall that lead to the devil.

The money I made neither did me nor my dear family any good. We thought it did, but no. You can see what it has done—a death sentence by hanging—and a broken-hearted family.

On the morning of August 17, the rumrunner breakfasted on four strips of bacon, two poached eggs, bread and coffee. Six carloads of guards followed him east to the shore road and south to the Coast Guard base, where wire had been strung to keep out devotees of the Gulf Stream Pirate, now just a godly man about to meet his maker.

Just after 6:00 a.m., surrounded by heavily armed guards, Alderman climbed up a hastily built rough pine scaffold at the Coast Guard hangar. Palm Beach County sheriff Bob Baker was recruited to apply the noose.

Of the survivors of the bloody shootout at sea, only one, Coast Guardsman Frank Tuten, watched the Gulf Stream Pirate die.

As Alderman left the jail, crowds of followers sang hymns, and Alderman continued singing one until the moment the floor dropped from under him. The rope failed to snap his neck, and he slowly strangled for some twelve minutes.

"His choking struggles could be heard for two minutes within the gray light of early dawn," one report said.

Alderman was the last man officially hanged in Florida's Broward County and the first man ever formally hanged by the U.S. Coast Guard.

As government was less open in the 1920s, the press was barred from the execution. The cops reporter for the *Miami Herald* had an idea. He made a deal with the undertaker to drive the hearse that would carry Alderman's corpse. But then he realized that everyone would recognize him. So the newspaper's amusements editor, Edgar Lee Hay, was recruited instead.

The *Herald*'s publisher, fearing a contempt-of-court rap—and as a personal favor to his college classmate, Judge Ritter—spiked the story. Hay fed his account to an Associated Press reporter, but that man's boss nixed it as well.

The *Herald* police reporter who had first planned to sneak in was Henry Reno, whose daughter Janet later became U.S. attorney general.

Starting in early 1928, no doubt shaken by the Alderman massacre, the Coast Guard beefed up its fleet in South Florida, acknowledged as the front line in the war on hooch. It sent down three thousand new men, twelve ships and the newest weapon: two seaplanes with radios.

But by 1933, the noble experiment had been pretty much declared a failure, and Prohibition ended. The new boogeymen would be the Great Depression and a great war.

Coast Guard Base 6 shut down after World War II and was sold to the City of Fort Lauderdale for $504,775. It is now the Bahia Mar Resort and Marina.

More than seven thousand people attended the four-hour funeral of the Gulf Stream Pirate. The dear departed, who was buried at a now-unmarked grave at Miami Memorial Park, wore a light suit, a white shirt and an orchid bow tie.

A reporter wrote, "His sharp-featured, twisted face bore a queer, faint smile."

Expanded from an article originally published in the *Palm Beach Post*, August 5, 2007.

Shootout on Old Dixie

"The Real Killer is the Man at the Small End of the Bottle"

A chill hung in the air, and the last slivers of the sun were red behind the stucco homes that lined the gravel two-lane Dixie Highway. The last of the commuters were chugging their way south, from downtown toward the newer neighborhoods on the edge of town; the neighborhoods that had sprung up seemingly within hours during the boom but that now, in the growing economic hard times, were a patchwork of lit and darkened bungalows crisscrossed by dirt roads and roughly carved canals.

One car was going north.

The old 1925 black beauty, one tire low and smoke spewing from the tailpipe, lurched to a stop at the corner of Dixie and Belvedere. Bob Moncure, a six-foot, one-inch, 265-pound bull, pushed open the driver's door.

Frank Patterson stretched a foot to the gravel and slid out the passenger's side. He pushed back his fedora and smoothed his twenty-dollar black suit.

Two more federal agents got out of the car. The four men walked toward 2403 South Dixie Highway.

Moncure's piece was in its holster on his hip. He had only one thing in his hand: a search warrant.

Robert Moncure, federal Prohibition agent slain in West Palm Beach by an alleged rumrunner. *Moncure family*.

The house a few hundred feet up was quiet, but a light shone from a side window. Inside, George Moore sat in his kitchen. In his lap, he cradled a shotgun.

Moncure knew the real estate. Three times already the Prohibition agent and his colleagues had raided George Moore's haunts, and one time they had nabbed 180 cases of hooch right at this home. Another time, they confiscated more than two thousand quarts. But Moore's slippery lawyers had been good. Real good. The bootlegger had beaten the rap.

This time, though, a snitch had tipped the feds that Moore had sold him thirteen quarts of whiskey. That was enough for a Prohibition commissioner to order a search. But Moore also had warned the feds about what might happen if they came to his house.

Moncure and Patterson didn't breathe a word. Their eyes did all the talking. The two silently stepped toward Moore's house.

Lisa Moncure, widow of slain federal Prohibition agent Robert Moncure. *Moncure family.*

Moncure motioned Patterson and W.M. McNulty to the back door. He went toward the front with James Kugler. Moncure's bulk made the porch's wooden floorboards creak. He took a step forward.

It was 5:56 p.m. on January 18, 1930.

Moncure stood on the porch in front of a wire screen door and rang the bell. George Moore came to stand on the other side of the screen. The agent held out a document.

"Moore, I have a federal search warrant for your home. Open the door and let us search."

"Nope."

Moore turned, threw open the wooden front door to the home and slammed it behind him. The door had a glass pane at about eye level.

Moncure wrestled with the screen door and jerked it open. He took several brisk steps to the front door.

The door shattered in a spray of wood. Moncure's face seemed to explode, and he flew back as if struck by a giant fist. He fell on the porch, unmoving. His eyes stared up at nothing.

Patterson heard the blast. He pushed through the back door and into the house.

Up front, George Moore stood just inside the tattered front door. Haze hung around his head and in the hallway behind him, along with the smell of gunpowder, hot metal and gore.

"Look out, George! He's going to shoot you!" came a voice. It was Merna Moore.

Her husband wheeled. He saw part of the profile of Patterson, standing in his kitchen, a hand reaching for a sidearm. Moore swung the shotgun up and fired through a kitchen cabinet. A giant red splotch instantly bloomed on Patterson's pressed white shirt as he went backward and sprawled on the floor.

Around the cabinet, Moore could see part of Patterson's body and his eyes, and he could hear him groan. Moore sat down. He could hear his own steady breathing and the muffled grinding of the Fords chugging by outside. The sun was gone now, and the house stood in growing shadow.

Out back, McNulty heard the second blast. He looked through the open door and stared at a shotgun pointing at him.

Merna fainted. Her young daughter, Olive, began pulling her up the stairs, bumping her limp body at each step. Moore raced over and helped Olive half carry, half drag Merna to the second floor.

The kitchen clock ticked.

After a few minutes, Moore heard the dim but growing whine of a police siren. It undulated up the scale, then down and then up again. It got louder. Then he heard a squeal of brakes on tires. The whine slowly died down.

It was 6:17 p.m. Nineteen minutes had passed.

A Ferguson ambulance was out front. Behind it was another West Palm Beach police car.

The springs of West Palm Beach police chief Frank Matthews's car creaked as he slid off the front seat and stood up in the street. He looked across the car's roof and spotted Moncure's large bulk lying motionless on the porch. His chest tightened.

The police chief walked slowly to Kugler and then past him. He walked to the side and the back of the house and returned to the front porch. He stepped across Big Bob's body. He looked down and saw the warrant lying in the man's blood.

Matthews stood there for a minute; then his chin came up and he saw the door, its wood splintered with a giant hole in the middle. Through it, in the darkness, he could barely make out the hallway, empty except for a dark, unmoving shape on the floor far to the back.

Matthews pulled off his hat and breathed out heavily. He turned and looked at the two uniforms standing on the sidewalk, their hands poised at their holsters. He turned back to the front door. He stepped inside.

"George. George Moore. Come on out," the chief said calmly but sternly.

A beat.

"Come upstairs, chief," he heard.

Matthews walked slowly up the stairs. With each step, more of Moore came into view. The man was holding the shotgun, muzzle pointed away from Matthews.

"Give me the gun, George," the chief said.

"Nope," Moore responded.

"C'mon, George."

"Chief, people I didn't know were breaking into my home. I was defendin' it."

Downstairs, detectives found where the screen door at the garage entrance to the home had been forced. Inside, a uniform kneeled before Patterson. The agent was half sitting, half leaning. He was unconscious. A .45-caliber pistol was next to his body.

"He's still alive!" the officer shouted.

The Ferguson's workers rushed to Patterson and carried him out front to the ambulance. The siren's whine grew fainter as the Ferguson raced toward Good Samaritan Hospital. The ambulance passed another car that pulled to the front of Moore's house. Out stepped Palm Beach County sheriff Bob Baker.

"I'm in here!" Chief Matthews shouted. "Stay out there, sheriff."

Baker stood and waited. The city detectives had arrived and were already on their hands and knees on the porch with sketch pads and measuring tapes.

Baker looked at his watch. It had been nearly twenty minutes.

Matthews was coming out the back door with Moore. He led the man toward a patrol car.

Moore knew the routine. He held out his hands behind his back and turned around. The cop slapped the cuffs hard, and they snapped shut with a click. He clamped a hand onto Moncure's horizontal forearm and led him around and off the porch. At the patrol car, the cop placed his hand on the top of Moore's head and lowered it, and him, inside.

The door slammed. The car made a U-turn and headed north toward downtown.

Back on the porch, Chief Matthews turned toward the sheriff.

"What a mess. I knew it would come to this. I knew it!"

The sheriff gingerly lifted the warrant and held it by a corner.

"What's gonna happen to the diner? And the boy. This'll kill him."

He sighed. "Who's gonna tell Liza?"

On January 18, 1930, two federal Prohibition agents died in an explosion of rage. While the preceding introduction made some educated guesses about dialogue and minor details, the events of January 18, 1930, and their aftermath, took place mostly as described here.

Today, the home is a shop where customers load up on Hoffman's chocolates, and the strongest words heard are usually about the never-ending construction on the road out front.

If you think of Prohibition, you might think of romantic images of flashy gangsters and gallant lawmen. But the battle was real, and it had real victims. Bob Moncure, Frank Patterson, George Moore, Frank Matthews and Bob Baker were real people.

At a time when Prohibition sometimes turned villains into heroes and heroes into villains, a jury cleared Moore on an astonishing technicality, and citizens cheered the result.

What follows is what happened to Bob Moncure's family after that fateful showdown on Dixie Highway.

Jack-Booted Thugs

In 1927, the U.S. Treasury Department created the Bureau of Prohibition Agents to enforce the Volstead Act. Not surprisingly, many agents were assigned to South Florida. One was Bob Moncure.

Born in Fredericksburg, Virginia, he was a sailor and merchant marine in the Great War and had been a truck farmer in Florida. He spent a total of three years with the agency, including a year's apprenticeship in Washington. He officially became a "dry man" in March 1929. He had lived in Jupiter and now lived in Lake Worth. He also owned the Washington Inn, at Lucerne and K Streets. His father was a judge in Alexandria, Virginia, and was a close friend of James H. Doran, the federal commissioner of Prohibition enforcement.

Moncure was forty-three. He had a teenage boy, Robert Knox Moncure Jr., nicknamed Knox.

Moncure knew that "dry men" were not popular. They were the "jack-booted thugs" of their time, enforcing a law that many people despised. Often, as in Vietnam, the public's ire for unpopular policies came down on the foot soldiers, on people like Bob Moncure. And in this upside-down time, rumrunners and bootleggers were glorified for getting around the law and getting the people what they wanted.

But these were not victimless crimes. Bob Moncure knew it. About 1927, a cousin, Prohibition agent Charles Rouse, had been killed during a raid in Baltimore. And Bob knew that peril could come unexpectedly. Once, during a raid at an illegal still, he had been severely scalded on the leg when he fell into a vat of steaming mash.

Frank Patterson joined the agency in July 1927, starting as a typist in Atlanta. He became an agent in April 1928 and came to South Florida from Atlanta about the same time as Moncure. He had a wife and four children. They lived on Avenida Allegre, about a mile from where Franklin Patterson would die.

George W. Moore came from Jacksonville to Palm Beach County about 1925. He lived at the home near Dixie Highway and Belvedere Road with his wife, Merna, thirty-five, and four daughters: Alilia, sixteen; Olive, fourteen; Merna, twelve; and Margaret, five.

Moore supplied the illicit alcohol for the Boca Raton Resort and Club and selected establishments in Palm Beach. Born about 1891, he hadn't touched the stuff himself until he was thirty-two. That was about 1923, soon after Prohibition began.

Moncure's grandson, Bob Moncure III, is an insurance agent in Boca Raton. He tells a family story, unconfirmed, that Moore tried to bribe Moncure with a new Packard if he would be sure he was in Boca Raton on a day when Moore would be coming into Jupiter Inlet. But Moncure reportedly said, "Mr. Moore, if I took your automobile, I never would have been able to drive it without looking in the rear-view mirror."

In the middle of January 1930, a snitch named Burton Arnold let the feds know that he had bought thirteen quarts of whiskey from Moore. They took his story to U.S. commissioner Robert L. Earnest. Earnest signed the search warrant.

On Saturday, January 18, the agents headed toward Moore's home. The night before, Bob and Liza Moncure had celebrated their seventeenth wedding anniversary.

"Cold-Blooded Murder"

Pat J. Lytal was four years old. He was standing on his porch. He saw a car parked in front of his house.

"I heard them shooting back and forth," Lytal, a longtime auto broker and a nephew of former Palm Beach County commissioner Lake Lytal, recently recalled. "There were guys scrambling around. There were a couple of guys behind the car. My grandmother grabbed me and pulled me inside."

The page for January 18, 1930, in the West Palm Beach police blotter shows that a Ferguson Ambulance was called at 6:17 p.m. to respond to a report of federal officers down. Chief Matthews was notified at his home a half minute later.

A police captain named Williams raced to the home and found Moncure dead. Patterson died on the table at Good Samaritan. Dr. L.A. Peck examined the bodies of the two men.

The next day, Liza Moncure opened her door for a reporter from the *New York Times.*

"My boy has lost a kind, wise, indulgent father, (and) his country has lost a conscientious, courageous and tireless fighter in the greatest war of all time," she declared. "My mother has lost a son, tender, affectionate and generous. I have lost…" She paused.

"Oh, what have I not lost? A protector. A pal for the past 17 years."

Then she continued:

> *Yet, if the eyes of this so blind country could be opened, if the dry-voting, wet-living congressmen could be made to realize the conditions as they are, if the corrupt judges who encourage these men by taking advantage of every technicality available to release them could be impeached, I would face my broken home and my joyless future with calm resignation and feel my ruined life a small price to pay.*

Supervisors from Washington, Jacksonville and Savannah raced to South Florida.

"I brought Moncure into the Prohibition service several years ago," Prohibition chief James Doran said. "He was a fine, clean chap and an efficient, honest officer."

The commissioner said that the deaths of Moncure and Patterson were "due in a large part to recent inflammatory attacks upon our personnel which leads weak-minded criminals to attack honest and efficient officers acting in the performance of their sworn duty."

But Moore's lawyers were already talking as well. And they were talking about, of all things, the clock.

Lawyers said that Moore was justified in shooting the agents because they had conducted an illegal search. They said it was illegal because the warrant did not state that liquor had been sold at the residence, it did not include the name of the informant and it was not an original document but a copy.

Moore's lawyer, E.M. Baynes, said that agents "broke into the house" and "some of the officers shouted, 'Shoot him.' Moore fired in self-defense."

He said that Moore had no knowledge that the officers had a search warrant. He said that Moore had warned the feds about improper searches and added, "The officers simply overstepped their bounds."

Robert Tuttle, administrator for the Prohibition agency district headquartered in Savannah, was not moved. "There can be no doubt that Moore well knew Agent Moncure when he visited his home on Saturday evening armed with a legal search warrant for execution on Moore's premises."

On Tuesday, January 21, at the Ferguson chapel, a double funeral took place at 5:00 p.m., as the day's last light was starting to fade.

Liza Moncure took her son and her husband's body to Washington, the Moncure family's home. Moncure was eventually buried at Arlington National Cemetery: section 17, grave 21561.

Patterson's widow took him and their four small children to Tampa.

On Wednesday, the twenty-second, a coroner's jury was impaneled in West Palm Beach.

A worker at a service station across the street and about one hundred feet to the south testified that he heard shouts after the first shot. The second shot was about fifteen seconds later, he said. One man told the coroner's jury that several weeks earlier he had been in a drugstore and overheard Moore threaten Prohibition agents if they didn't stay away from his place.

"This isn't about whether you like or dislike the 18th Amendment or what the proper conduct of officers should be," Prohibition bureau legal adviser A.S. Anderson told the coroner's jury. "No evidence has been submitted that Moore asked to see the warrant or find out if there was any warrant. On top of that, Moore knew agent Moncure. This was cold-blooded murder."

The jury also brought in famed Palm Beacher Gus Jordahn, owners of Gus's Baths. The gruff but lovable Scandinavian had his own weather station. He testified that he had calculated official sunset on January 18 at 5:52 p.m.

The clock.

After two days of hearings and deliberations, the coroner's jury ruled that George Moore should be charged with murder. Liza Moncure swore out a formal complaint for her husband and another for his partner.

In February, Delray Beach Reverend Frank H. Nelson, editor of a publication called *Sky Talk*, blamed the deaths on apathy and winking support for bootleggers. In an article he said the "secular press" refused to publish, he wrote, "No law can be enforced when the public conscience is dead."

Too many champaigne [sic] shakers and whiskey toppers know that THEY WERE RESPONSIBLE for Patterson's and Moncure's death. The man who makes the bootlegger necessary is the man who knifes the enforcers of law. The real killer is the man at the small end of the bottle.

Pastor Nelson railed about the tears shed over the 135 bootleggers killed since the start of Prohibition, while "little sympathy was given the widows and orphans of 58 officers of the law who fell in line of duty. These men were killed intentionally. Patterson and Moncure make 60."

And in Washington, former New York mayor Fiorello La Guardia, then a U.S. congressman, told a House debate on the slayings that bootleggers could not operate with such impunity "if there were not thousands of law-abiding citizens resenting Prohibition and ready to buy their wares."

At 10:00 a.m. on January 30, Moore posted $10,000 bond and walked out of the county jail. In March, a local grand jury issued two indictments. They were for second-degree murder, which meant that the panel believed Moore should be charged with shooting the two in the heat of the moment and not with premeditation.

But what about the clock?

Moore was tried first for the death of Bob Moncure. The names of one hundred local citizens—all men—were pulled for what was then one of the largest jury pools ever in Palm Beach County.

The trial started on April 21.

On the morning of April 23, Olive Moore took the stand. The fourteen-year-old said that she had been on the couch in the living room with her parents when she heard a disturbance at the front door, and her father stood up to investigate.

At 11:00 a.m., George W. Moore testified.

"I heard a noise at the back door and then one at the front door. No one rang the doorbell."

Later, he said, "I did not recognize either of the men I shot. I did not realize they were agents until Chief Matthews told me."

Then there was the time element.

The search warrant had been for daytime only. Bob Moncure had stood on George Moore's stoop at 5:56 p.m. Sunset had officially come at 5:52 p.m. In those four minutes, Moore's lawyers argued, their warrant had become invalid, and they had gone from officers of the law to unknown trespassers threatening a citizen, his property and his family.

Prosecutors scoffed.

Official or not, it wasn't dark yet. Besides, they said, Moore knew Moncure all too well. The agent had helped raid his home at least once before. On top of that, Moncure had identified himself and held the search warrant for the bootlegger to see.

Both sides waived final arguments, and the judge gave the jurors the case.

"A man is within his rights in defending his home to the extent of killing another person, especially when he believes that his home, family or himself will be injured," Judge A.G. Hartridge intoned in his charge to the jury. "You should acquit the defendant if you find the agents went to the Moore residents after sundown with a daytime search warrant, which is invalid after nightfall, and were found to be trespassing on Mr. Moore's property."

Jurors retired at 2:36 p.m. They were back at the stroke of 3:00 p.m. They had been gone twenty-four minutes.

Hartridge warned the audience against demonstrations, and then the verdict was announced: not guilty.

Cheers rang out. The judge ordered a deputy to find and arrest those responsible. But none could be found.

"To Suddenly Know HATE"

Moore knew that his problems weren't over.

On July 17, 1930, county prosecutors dropped the murder charge for Patterson. But Moore was later indicted on a federal charge of assaulting a federal officer in connection with Patterson's death. Trial was to take place in Miami.

Liza sat down and wrote a letter to her dead husband. She wrote that she went to Miami for the trial, and there, in the marshal's office, she ran into the man who had killed her beloved Bob.

> *O my darling, how did I keep from rushing in and tearing him apart with my bare hands. Why is it that my miserable body turns so weak and ill every time I see him. I don't believe I could speak a word to him to save my life. It is a terrible thing to have arrived at my age without ever knowing hate, and then to suddenly know HATE! It is so devastating.*

George Moore was convicted in federal court and sentenced to ten years. The federal judge ruled that, although the search warrant had been presented past official sunset, it was still light enough for people to see features. In April 1932, an appeals court upheld the conviction.

Moore was sent to the federal prison in Atlanta.

In May 1935, Moore was cleared on a separate federal liquor conspiracy charge along with two codefendants. The men had been charged with conspiring to bring a boatload of liquor to shore three miles north of Jupiter in 1927. But two government witnesses were charged with perjury. The judge said that they "apparently have been tampered with."

Moore eventually was released from prison. He moved his family to a home on Upland Street in West Palm Beach, near his former house.

Moore died in May 1958. He was sixty-seven. He left behind his wife, Merna, four daughters, eight grandchildren and three great-grandchildren. A three-paragraph obituary lists his occupation as owner of a roofing and painting company.

Merna died in 1975. Three of their four daughters have since died, leaving only the youngest, Margaret, now Margaret Briant.

"He never talked about it. Not around any of us," Margaret, then eighty, said in 2004 from Leesburg, where she had moved about twelve years earlier. "He kept that stuff strictly away from the family. It wasn't discussed at home."

That didn't stop Margaret's classmates from taunting her with "You're a jailbird's daughter."

"I have no recollection of the incident itself," Briant said. All her dad would ever say, she recalled, is this: "When they were entering the house, they were entering the kingdom."

Liza Moncure died in 1968 at age seventy-five. She never remarried.

The Moncures' son, Knox, became an engineer for the U.S. Army. He retired to Port St. Lucie. His son, Robert III, said that Knox could not come back to West Palm Beach because the memories were too painful. Knox died in 1993.

In her letter to her dead husband in the summer of 1930, Liza wrote that she had visited a family retreat:

> *Words can not describe my feelings as I unlocked that door to Memory Lane. The time your leg was burned in the boiling mash and you thought— we both thought you would lose it. How admirable you were.*
>
> *How could I have been so unconscious of this horrible ax over my head. I went in the front room where the night blooming jessamine used to intoxicate us with its sweetness. What memories! So sweet, so dear, they almost overshadow the bitterness of now.*

Liza wrote that James Kugler, the agent who had gone to the front porch with her husband and who had watched him die, told her, "Think how much you have to be thankful for in the memories you have of him and the replica you have of him in Knox, who is getting to be a man now and who needs your encouragement to carry on and be the kind of man Bob would have him be."

And, she wrote, "another time he [Kugler] said, 'somehow, things have never been the same since the 18th of Jan. There is not the same spirit of brotherhood in the men as there used to be when Bob was here. Somehow, I can't get over expecting them to come back.' Dear God!"

At the end of the typewritten letter, Liza handwrote a note to her in-laws in Virginia, where Knox was staying. She told them to use their judgment about whether to show the letter to the boy, adding, "For a long time, I used to write letters to Bob. Somehow, it seemed to comfort me."

Near the end of the typed part, Liza said she had a dream in which she had run to the office to have lunch with Robert. It was payday.

> *We started out to the elevator and you called back, "so long, fellows. When I come back I will be a picked bird." We went out to the laughter of the whole office and I ran down the steps holding your hand. When I woke up, the cruelty of the whole awakening almost killed me. Honey, it literally almost killed me. I can't cry yet, but I felt like—like I was bleeding to death. I just lay still while waves of dispair [sic] engulfed me. HOW can I go on living with this terrible load of sorrow that does not grow any lighter. Other women lose their husbands, but not such a husband. And not such a woman whose life was bound up in her home.*
>
> *God help me. God help me.*

Expanded from articles originally published in the *Palm Beach Post*, January 23, 1995, and January 16, 2005.

Snowbird Gangsters

Did gangsters Al Capone and John Dillinger ever hang out in Palm Beach County?

Capone mostly hung out in Miami, but he was not particularly loved there, and a news report from 1930 places him in Palm Beach County, perhaps eyeing real estate; another says that a lawyer bought a Boca Raton tract for him.

He reportedly had an option on a fifty-six-acre island in the Hillsboro Canal, south of Boca Raton on the Broward County side. Long called "Capone Island," it is now Deerfield Island Park. The state took it in 1934 when Capone went bankrupt. "Scarface" went to prison and then lived out his later years, racked with syphilis, at his home on ritzy Palm Island, near Miami. He died at age forty-eight in 1947.

Unlike Capone, who ruled Chicago's underworld for years, Dillinger spent only fourteen months in the headlines, committing crimes mostly across the

Gangster Al Capone. Palm Beach Post *archives*.

Midwest and West. He hit the road after a gang member killed a policeman in Chicago, and in late 1933 and early 1934, he was placed in the West Palm Beach area, where the gang reportedly rented a beach house.

One story had gang members hearing fireworks exploding on New Year's Eve and joining in by wildly firing their machine guns.

On July 22, 1934, as Dillinger left Chicago's Biograph Theatre, he was gunned down by law officers who were waiting for him. He was thirty-one.

Sellers's House and Farm, a two-room home built about 1922 on pioneer Perry Sellers's pig farm west of Lake Worth, reportedly hosted Dillinger. The home is sometimes called "the Dillinger House." It is now on display at Yesteryear Village at the South Florida Fairgrounds in suburban West Palm Beach.

According to Claudia Alter at Yesteryear, the home was built in 1927 west of Military Trail on South Lake Worth Road. The Sellerses were sharecroppers and also ran a small pig farm. They raised six children in the tiny two-room house, with no running water or inside plumbing.

Gangster John Dillinger. Palm Beach Post *archives*.

Reportedly, Perry and his wife, Josephine, were close friends of gangster John Dillinger, and while hiding from lawmen, he stayed at their home in the 1930s and spent his days hunting alligators.

The building was donated by the Sellerses' son Arthur and was moved to Yesteryear Village in June 1992. It now sports a small farm in back, growing cotton, tobacco, rice, corn, tomatoes and other crops, along with a flower and butterfly garden and a collection of chickens and ducks.

Other period buildings at Yesteryear include:

L Street House: A 1925 bungalow that was moved from Lake Worth. It has seven-foot ceilings, several small rooms and a "sleeping porch," a front room with windows that families slept in during hot summer nights.

Hospitality House: Also built in 1925, it was moved from Old Okeechobee Boulevard, near the Kravis Center, about 1999 and is used by volunteers.

Telephone Museum: This 1930s Lake Worth home was restored using a 1930s photograph of a Miami telephone office as a resource; equipment was donated by local telephone pioneers' organizations.

The following are some replica buildings actually reconstructed with wood from the village's working sawmill:

Smoke House: Used to smoke meats for sale at the village.
Saloon: Built in 2002 to replicate a 1920s saloon. Sorry, root beer only.
Jail: Built in 1999. The jail door is real.
Gazebo: Built about 2000, not from the village's sawmill lumber but from a "kit"; it replicates the old band shell that often stood in the center of a town and is used for various events.

You can contact Yesteryear Village at (561) 795-3110 or visit their website at www.southfloridafair.com/html/yesteryearvillage.html.

Originally published in the *Palm Beach Post*, February 19, 2003; March 5, 2003; November 26, 2003; and January 21, 2004.

Son of Al Capone

"I Love that Kid"

When Albert Francis Jr. died at age eighty-five on July 8, 2004, in the small northern California town of Auburn Lake Trails, his obituary in the local newspaper mentioned his years in the area, his education in South Florida, funeral arrangements and surviving relatives.

What it did not mention was that Albert had changed his name and lived most of his life in obscurity to escape his family shame. He had, to most of the outside world, carried his secret to his grave: he was born Albert Francis Capone Jr.

"Al Capone has been dead a long, long time," widow America Francis said by telephone in June 2005. "His son had nothing to do with him. Let him rest in peace, for crying out loud. He suffered enough in his life for being who he was."

Alphonse Capone was more than a sometime snowbird in Palm Beach County and South Florida. The gangster nicknamed "Scarface" reportedly bought a large ranch in Jupiter Farms in 1923 that was later purchased by Burt Reynolds. Capone bought a palatial home in Palm Island, an exclusive community near downtown Miami, but was reportedly considering property in Boca Raton after Miami authorities and community leaders let him know that he wasn't welcome. He supposedly had an option on a fifty-six-acre

Sonny Capone, son of gangster Al Capone, at his wedding. *Historical Museum of Southern Florida*.

island in the Hillsboro Canal, south of Boca Raton on the Broward County side. Long called "Capone Island," it is now Deerfield Island Park. The state took it in 1934 when Capone went bankrupt.

The man considered to be one of the most ruthless gangsters in American history had a soft spot for his son. "I don't want to die shot in the street," he once said. "There's business enough for all of us without killing each other like animals. I've got a boy. I love that kid."

"Sonny" was born on December 4, 1918, in Brooklyn, the son of Capone's Irish wife, Mae Coughlin. At age seven, he developed an infection in his mastoid, the bone behind his ear. The family consulted specialists in New York. Sonny survived the radical surgery but was left partially deaf and had to wear a hearing aid.

His deafness, coupled with his infamous surname, caused him no end of trouble with classmates, and he bounced from one school to another. He attended St. Patrick School in Miami Beach, where he was good friends with a young Cuban named Desi Arnaz. Sonny attended Notre Dame University from 1937 to 1938 and then returned to South Florida, where he received a bachelor's degree from the University of Miami in 1941.

Sonny married Ruth Casey in Miami in 1941. The two had four daughters. They later divorced and Sonny remarried. A brother-in-law was a Miami police detective, and Sonny met other officers. He was an expert marksman and joined the department's pistol team, becoming a member of the National Pistol Association of America and the Florida Peace Officers' Association.

His father, meanwhile, had been sentenced in 1932 to an eleven-year term for tax evasion that would include stints in Atlanta and Los Angeles and at San Francisco's infamous Alcatraz prison. Capone served only seven years before he was released, his body racked with syphilis.

In 1942, when applying for an aviation school, Sonny listed his father's occupation as "retired." And he was there when Scarface died at his Palm Island home at age forty-eight on January 19, 1947.

Sonny's first job after World War II was as a used car salesman. But the son of an underworld legend quit after learning that his boss was turning back the odometers on the cars. He became an apprentice printer and hoped to buy into the business, but his mother declined to back him.

For a while, the two ran a Miami restaurant called the Grotto, with Sonny as head waiter, but it eventually closed.

He and his mother lived quietly until 1959, when they filed a $1 million lawsuit against the producers of *The Untouchables*. The TV series detailed the exploits of 1930s Chicago cop Eliot Ness and was groundbreaking and controversial for what was then considered excessive violence. The family claimed that the show was using Capone's image for profit. The Federal Communications Commission reprimanded ABC, but the family eventually lost the suit. The show's producer was Sonny's childhood friend, Desi Arnaz.

On August 7, 1965, the son of the great mob boss found himself picked up like a common criminal. Police said he had pocketed two bottles of aspirin and flashlight batteries, totaling $3.50, from a North Miami Beach supermarket. He reportedly said, "Everyone has a little larceny in them."

Sonny, then living in Hollywood and working as a tire distributor, pleaded no contest and was sentenced to two years probation. When it was lifted in 1967, his probation officer said that he had been exemplary, and the store manager said he had been a steady—and paying—customer.

There was one thing that Sonny was no longer: Albert Francis Capone Jr. The previous year, he had gone to court in Fort Lauderdale and had his name legally changed to Albert Francis. His lawyer said that he was "just getting sick and tired of fighting the name." Sonny was forty-seven, about the same age his father had been when he died.

By then, all four of his daughters were living in California. Sometime in the 1980s, records show, Sonny moved there as well, living in Los Altos, between San Francisco and San Jose, and later in Cool, a small community northeast of Sacramento. In 1988, at age seventy, he took a three-week African safari with friends.

At his death, on July 8, 2004, he left behind his four daughters and numerous grandchildren and great-grandchildren. Well-wishers were asked to donate to the Alzheimer's Association. Services were private.

Originally published in the *Historical Association of Southern Florida Magazine* (Summer 2008). Reprinted here with permission.

Hoagy in Palm Beach

The young clerk was working at his desk in a West Palm Beach law firm when he heard a familiar tune wafting up to his open window. He leaped from his chair and ran down to the street and around the corner to a nearby music shop.

They were playing his song.

"That's 'Washboard Blues'! My 'Washboard,'" the clerk recalled shouting years later. "At the music store, I stood panting, sweating, watching a record go around, trying to read the name on it, going cross-eyed. Finally, it stopped. It was a record of 'Washboard Blues' that I hadn't known had been made. By Red Nichols. I bought the only copy in the shop. I played it again and again."

Pretty soon, Hoagland Carmichael, the writer of "Washboard Blues" and struggling clerk in the law offices of a former West Palm Beach mayor, was out of the legal business and into the music business.

"Washboard" has been all but forgotten, but so many of Hoagy Carmichael's songs remain part of American popular culture: "Georgia on My Mind," "Lazy River," "The Nearness of You." More than seventy-five years ago, his most famous tune, the haunting melody "Stardust," was first recorded. And for seventy-five years, a myth has built around the song and its supposed origins in Palm Beach County.

It was always believed that Murray Carmichael, Hoagy's employer at the West Palm law firm, was Hoagy's uncle and that Hoagy wrote "Stardust" while gazing across the Intracoastal Waterway at Murray's home, which is now the site of the First Baptist Church of West Palm Beach at 1101 South Flagler Drive.

Hoagy Carmichael was a law student in West Palm Beach. Palm Beach Post *archives*.

"The family story is that he wrote it down on some paper on the front porch," said Charles Fulton, Murray Carmichael's grandson and an Episcopal priest and president of a national ministry based in Atlanta.

Douglas Carmichael Fulton, Charles's younger brother and an assistant Palm Beach County state's attorney for nineteen years, never met Hoagy. But on occasions when Hoagy was on television, he said, "My mother would drag us in really quick, and say, 'He wrote at our house.'"

Hoagy might have written there, but it wasn't "Stardust," says his son.

"He wrote it in law school [in Indiana]," Hoagy B. Carmichael, Hoagy's son, said in an interview from New York.

Too many colleagues at the school recalled hearing the song when it "was beginning to sound like something," he said. "What I'm positive of was that it was not written in 46 other homes that I've heard it was written [in]. West Palm Beach was not where that song got its genesis, trust me. He may have played it in West Palm Beach, and people may have heard it in West Palm Beach, and people may have thought it was wonderful in West Palm Beach."

It also turns out that, despite a shared last name and both being from Indiana, Murray Carmichael and Hoagy Carmichael aren't related.

"To my surprise, the records in Indiana don't show that we're related, which contradicts the whole family story," Fulton said. "It's obviously disappointing, because we've always been proud of that connection, but we always like the truth."

Fulton and others should be forgiven for taking everything Hoagy said at face value, the songwriter's son said with a bit of a sigh. "Never trust completely the intricacies of my father's stories, because they ended up sometimes—not always, but sometimes—having a life of their own."

"Hoagy was never one to let an inconvenient fact stand between him and a good yarn," added Richard M. Sudhalter, author of the Hoagy biography *Stardust Melody*. "His memoirs abound with stories that just when you look at the factual record could not possibly be true."

No one disputes that Hoagy spent time in West Palm Beach as he wrestled with a major career decision: the law or music.

Born on November 22, 1899, in Bloomington, Indiana, Hoagy helped his family by playing piano for dances at Indiana University. He moved to Indianapolis in 1916 and then returned to Bloomington to attend the college, where he formed a jazz band.

After receiving a law degree from Indiana in 1926, he came down to boom-time South Florida, where he worked as a clerk for the Carmichael and Carmichael firm, led by Murray DuBoise Carmichael.

Murray Carmichael came to West Palm Beach from Indiana in 1910. He was elected to one-year terms as mayor in 1913, 1914 and 1921. He also was city and county attorney and spent two years in the Florida House of Representatives. His law office was at the Citizens Bank Building at 105 South Narcissus Avenue.

"I've stood in front of the building," said Hoagy's son.

Books by and about Hoagy shed little light on his brief stay in South Florida. In his two published memoirs, *The Stardust Road* and *Sometimes I Wonder*, he said that he earned fifty dollars a month as a law clerk, "free to choose among mule-kicking cases, collecting bad debts, shotgun weddings, orange grove escrows, wife beating, fishing contracts, land assessments [and] incorporation of fine companies by men with earnest smiles and no assets."

Hoagy said that he enjoyed the work until the 1920s real-estate boom collapsed. And when he got a last-minute gig playing drums on a cruise ship to Havana, the law office looked "duller than ever."

Hoagy left a song, "Washboard Blues," with publisher Irving Mills in New York. That's the song that he heard through the law office's window, performed by popular jazz cornetist Red Nichols and his Five Pennies.

The music store where the record was being played would have been Philpott's on Clematis Street, around the corner from the law office, according to Beryl B. Lewis, a *Palm Beach Post* employee for a half century.

"He was always at the keyboards just inside the store, trying to compose music," Lewis recalled in 1981 after Hoagy died of heart failure at Rancho Mirage, California.

In the 1920s, the *Post* newsroom—and Lewis's desk—were headquartered on Narcissus Avenue, close to Carmichael's law office.

Hoagy "was generally there at noon or late in the afternoon," said Lewis, who died in 1988. "At first, I didn't know who he was. I inquired a number of times from various persons, 'Who in the world was always at the keyboards?' Invariably the reply, if they thought they knew, was 'Hoagy Carmichael.'"

In his memoir, Hoagy said that after the music store encounter he walked back to his desk and wrote a letter to Red Nichols, saying, in part, "I am planning on leaving this tin-eared rendezvous of hunted bank presidents and screw drivers' union [*sic*] for points north." Soon he was back in Indiana, playing the music he loved.

Sudhalter says that Hoagy's departure wasn't all about a young rebel chasing his dreams. He has a letter that the Florida Bar sent Hoagy in June 1926, telling him that he had failed his bar exam. Sudhalter says that Murray Carmichael fired Hoagy.

While visiting friends and family in Indiana, Hoagy wrote in 1933 that "M.D. Carmichael pulled his purse strings tighter than ever (Lord knows they were tight enough) and the world lost a promising young attorney. The fact that my belongings were in West Palm Beach made no difference to him. I returned and stuck it out for a while, but the spirit was gone."

Hoagy didn't give up immediately, Sudhalter said. He returned to Indiana and passed that state's bar; he then worked for a while at an Indianapolis law firm. But soon he dove full time into songwriting.

Hoagy moved to New York in 1929 and later to California. He penned many memorable songs and even appeared in movies, most notably the Humphrey Bogart and Lauren Bacall classic *To Have and Have Not*. In 1971, Carmichael was one of ten charter members of the Songwriters Hall of Fame.

According to news reports, Hoagy came back to West Palm Beach over the years to visit his old haunts, and perhaps to watch the stars over the Intracoastal and remember the time a song through an open window changed the course of his life.

Originally published in the *Palm Beach Post*, September 14, 2003.

II

Palm Beach Past

ROARING PALM BEACH

Gershwin in Palm Beach

Q: Recently you wrote about famed songwriter Hoagy Carmichael's stint as a law clerk in West Palm Beach. Didn't the brilliant George Gershwin also write some of his great songs in Palm Beach?

To answer this question, I looked close to home, to Gershwin biographies and to veteran journalist and Gershwin lover Howard Kleinberg. My father wrote about the composer's Florida visits in a September 1998 *Miami Herald* column for what would have been Gershwin's 100th birthday.

As early as 1925, Gershwin's visits to Florida, and the public's fascination with the state's real-estate boom, inspired his Broadway musical *Tip-Toes*, set in Palm Beach.

Gershwin spent the winter of 1933 at a Palm Beach home on South Ocean Boulevard that oil tycoon Emil Mosbacher had rented with his wife and three children. It was there that Gershwin wrote variations on "I Got Rhythm." And in 1935, after studying black culture in Charleston, South Carolina, he returned to the island to write much of the groundbreaking opera *Porgy and Bess*.

"Palm Beach is once more itself after a few days of cold weather," the composer wrote to his brother and songwriting partner, Ira. "I'm sitting in the patio of the charming house Emil has rented, writing to you after orchestrating for a few hours this morning...it goes slowly, there being millions of notes to write."

Mosbacher later said in a Gershwin biography that Palm Beachers were constantly inviting the composer to their parties. He said that Gershwin often complained, but Mosbacher didn't buy it.

"He'd go, and play all night, and come home and complain like hell the next day," the millionaire said.

Legendary composer George Gershwin both played and worked in Palm Beach. Palm Beach Post *archives*.

Just two years later, in 1937, Gershwin died of a brain tumor. He was only thirty-eight.

Originally published in the *Palm Beach Post,* August 13, 2003.

Babe Ruth in Palm Beach

Spring training is legend in South Florida, so here's an item on a local visit by a baseball legend. On February 4, 1930, New York Yankees slugger Babe Ruth, vacationing in Palm Beach, rejected a two-year, $75,000-a-year contract and threatened to retire unless the Yankees gave him a three-year, $85,000-a-year deal. Ruth was then making $70,000. The team's manager and owner said it wasn't right to risk that much money on the uncertainties of baseball and on Ruth in particular.

Ruth sent sports editors a mimeographed, five-hundred-word tome. He said that one advertiser had paid him $1,000 three years earlier for a ten-minute radio talk and was now paying him $2,500. Given those figures, Ruth

Baseball legend Babe Ruth and friends at the Lake Worth Municipal Golf Course in 1925. Palm Beach Post *archives.*

Baseball legend Babe Ruth late in his career. Palm Beach Post *archives*.

said that he figured the Yankees should be paying him $175,000. Ruth said he was guaranteed $25,000 a year in royalties and dividends if he never played another inning.

"Today I am in fine physical shape," he wrote.

> *Golf, fishing and hunting have kept me trim since last October. During the winter I rejected easy money in vaudeville and talking pictures to keep myself in shape, but if the Yankees force me into retirement, I will accept one of the many offers which include a variety of entertainment propositions, exhibition games during the summer and even an offer from a circus.*

A month later, on March 8, the Babe signed a two-year, $80,000-a-year deal, $5,000 more than what President Herbert Hoover made. Ruth would later say, "I had a better year." It made Ruth the highest-paid player in baseball history. In today's dollars, it would be equivalent to $851,764.

But times have changed. The $25.2 million salary of New York Yankee Alex Rodriguez in 2005 means that Rodriguez earned $155,556 per game.

Originally published in the *Palm Beach Post*, March 1, 2006.

Downtown West Palm Beach's Boom-Time Buildings

Wayne Miner of Belle Glade, who grew up in West Palm Beach and sold copies of the *Palm Beach Post* for a nickel as a young man in the late 1950s and early '60s, wrote to ask the history of three downtown West Palm Beach landmark buildings: the Harvey, the Comeau and the Citizens.

The Citizens building, one of downtown West Palm Beach's early office buildings. Palm Beach Post *archives*.

A 1985 image of the 100,000-square-foot Comeau building, one of downtown West Palm Beach's early office buildings, at 319 Clematis Street. Palm Beach Post *archives*.

The L-shaped Harvey Building, at the southeast corner of Datura Street and South Olive Avenue, is a monument to South Florida's roaring 1920s real estate boom. It was built between 1925 and 1927. The original owner was Boston businessman George W. Harvey. The architect was Henry Steven Harvey. At fourteen stories, it was then the city's tallest structure. It and the Comeau dominated the downtown skyline into the 1980s.

Noted for its arcade and tower, the steel and brick edifice has an exterior of granite and eight-inch-thick Indiana limestone, as well as a marble foyer. It cost $1 million to build in 1920s dollars, which is the equivalent of about $11.6 million today. It hosted U-boat spotters during World War II and the area's first television station antenna in 1953. It is currently owned by David Associates and its chief executive officer, Alfred Marulli, a local real estate investor.

The ten-story Comeau building, at 319 Clematis Street, also designed by Henry Harvey's architecture firm, raced to open before the Harvey and won by days. Henry Harvey, meanwhile, was elected mayor.

Investor Albert Beriro bought the Comeau, the "grande dame of Clematis Street," for $4.5 million in 1999 and did extensive renovations, returning the huge chandeliers in the lobby to their original black and restoring the wall sconces. Beriro sold the building in the fall of 2006 to the New Chicago Partners investment group.

The third structure, the eight-story Citizens building, was built before the Harvey or the Comeau, in 1923, at the southwest corner of Clematis and Narcissus Streets, for the Citizens Investment company. The building staggered through foreclosure during the Depression and has gone through various owners.

Wayne should have mentioned the Guaranty building as well. The forty-thousand-square-foot structure, which opened in 1924, was also designed by architect Henry Stephen Harvey, a West Palm Beach mayor who worked on the Harvey and the now demolished Pennsylvania Hotel.

The Guaranty building is currently owned by the New Chicago Partners investment group, which also owns the Comeau.

Of the four buildings, two are on the National Register of Historic Places: the Comeau (listed September 9, 1996) and the Guaranty (listed December 10, 1998).

Special thanks go to Friederike Mittner, historic preservation planner for the city of West Palm Beach, and the owners and management of the four buildings, with the exception of RMC Florida, listed on property records as owner of the Citizens. The company refused to talk to us or confirm that it owns the place.

Originally published in the *Palm Beach Post*, January 31, 2007, and February 7, 2007.

West Palm Beach's Early Theatres and Boxing Venues

Longtime resident Roger St. Martin of suburban Lake Worth, who once was a pin boy at the Carefree bowling alley, asked for some details on the West Palm Beach area's early theatres and its boxing arena.

Former child actor Carl Kettler opened the Bijou, the city's first theatre, in 1908 on the southwest corner of where Clematis Street now splits. He later moved it to Clematis and Narcissus Streets and replaced it with the Kettler in 1924.

The Kettler cost $500,000, in 1920's dollars, and boasted fourteen seats, colored lights, fans and smoking rooms. It became the Palms and was razed in 1965.

The Florida Theatre opened in 1949 north of the Kettler. It closed in 1981, operated as a stage theatre until 1991, briefly reopened in 1996 and is now the Cuillo Centre for the Arts.

The Carefree Bowlaway, south of downtown, opened in 1939; it became the Carefree Theatre in 1948 and continued to present films and live shows. Its roof collapsed during Hurricane Wilma in 2005, and it remains closed.

The 1,068-seat Paramount Theatre in Palm Beach, showing major films and drawing top-name entertainers, operated from 1927 to 1968, reopened briefly and then was converted to a retail and office complex in 1982.

The Oakley Theatre, a Lake Worth vaudeville and movie house, opened in 1924. Damaged by the 1928 hurricane and victimized by the Depression, it was dark for decades, then reopened as an adult theatre in the 1970s and became the Lake Worth Playhouse in 1975. Cofounder Lucien Oakley supposedly haunts the place.

Now to boxing venues.

Early in the twentieth century, the West Palm Beach area was popular for small-club boxing, fueled by interest among winter visitors, including financier E.F. Hutton and others who sponsored "stables" of fighters.

The local American Legion held fights in an indoor arena built in the late 1920s on the north side of Clematis Street, near the Florida East Coast Railway crossing. Bleachers held as many as two thousand spectators. Palm Beachers bought private boxes that framed the ring.

Boxing on TV in the late 1940s killed local boxing everywhere, including in the West Palm Beach area.

One of the early club fighters was a strapping University of Florida student who won fifty-nine straight fights there and elsewhere and who, in

A postcard image of Clematis Street, downtown West Palm Beach. Palm Beach Post *archives*.

The interior of the Kettler Theatre. *Janet Bursey*.

1931, just three months before finishing law school, was tempted by a $685 purse to enter the ring at New York's Madison Square Garden.

His sixtieth opponent broke his jaw in the first round, but he struggled through all ten rounds. Later that year, he was elected a municipal judge in West Palm Beach. Phil O'Connell spent a quarter century as Palm Beach County state's attorney. He died in 1987.

Originally published in the *Palm Beach Post*, August 30, 2006, and September 6, 2006.

Dixie Highway

It might be interesting to look into the history of Dixie Highway in Palm Beach County.
—Paul Andres, suburban Palm Beach Gardens

Previous columns have covered the various manifestations of U.S. 1, of which Dixie Highway is sometimes a part, but not Dixie Highway itself. Inspired by the burgeoning automobile industry, business leaders began

An early 1920s image of Dixie Highway, at the county line between Palm Beach and St. Lucie Counties in Stuart. Martin County was created in 1925. Palm Beach Post *archives*.

pressing for better and more far-reaching roads and highways, including roads to the tourist destinations of Florida. One booster was Carl Fisher, founder of the Indianapolis 500 and the father of Miami Beach. Planning started in 1914. When finished in 1927, Dixie Highway stretched more than fifty-seven hundred miles from Ontario to Florida City.

Portions of the original highway that crossed into Florida were: Central Dixie Highway, Macon, Georgia, to Jacksonville; North Florida Connector, Tallahassee to Jacksonville; East Florida Connector, Hastings to Orlando; Central Florida Connector, Kissimmee to Melbourne; Scenic Highlands Highway, Haines City to Okeechobee; and South Florida Connector, Arcadia to West Palm Beach.

In South Florida, according to the website www.us-highways.com, Dixie Highway, sometimes called "Old Dixie," follows U.S. 1 to the Martin–Palm Beach county line and once followed the Florida East Coast Railway through Jonathan Dickinson State Park, but that segment is no longer drivable. Near Jupiter Lighthouse, it splits off U.S. 1 to become part of Alternate A1A (State Road 811) and then merges with U.S. 1 in West Palm Beach. It splits off and runs parallel to U.S. 1, starting in northern Delray Beach, and continues into Broward County.

Originally published in the *Palm Beach Post*, October 4, 2006.

Mail Boats to Lake Okeechobee

My granddad (deceased) Ernest Eugene Archer and my Uncle Elbert Hester (deceased) used to run the mail boat between Lake Harbor, Palm Beach and Okeechobee. Do you have any information on the mail boats? Would have probably been in the '30s, '40s or maybe '50s.

—Paula Garrard, Okeechobee

I checked with our archives, local historical societies and venerable Glades-area historian Joseph Orsenigo, all without luck. Orsenigo—who died in June 2009—did say at the time, "The mail boat era ended when rail and road networks were developed, probably before 1930."

We do know that boats, including mail boats, plied the West Palm Beach Canal from the lake to downtown West Palm Beach in the early part of the twentieth century. A stub canal connected to a basin at the current site of the pond at Howard Park, across from the Kravis Center. At the "turning basin," barges unloaded passengers and thousands of crates of Glades

In the late 1920s, a national Shriner's convention in Boca Raton encouraged city leaders to construct this giant camel. *Boca Raton Historical Society*.

produce. Some were transferred to railroad cars on a spur. The basin and canal lost favor for produce, passengers and mail when a railroad line and motor highway to the Glades opened in the mid-1920s. The 1928 hurricane destroyed the docks.

For additional research or information, contact the Belle Glade Library at (561) 996-3453 or the Historical Society of Palm Beach County at (561) 832-4164.

Originally published in the *Palm Beach Post*, May 9, 2007.

Downtown West Palm Beach, 1926, as seen from the old Pennsylvania Hotel. Palm Beach Post *archives*.

History of the Intracoastal Waterway

Many readers have asked questions relating to the Intracoastal Waterway. The following are some excerpts from a brief history of the waterway, written by David Roach, executive director of the Florida Inland Navigation District. It appeared in the summer 2003 edition of *Coastlines*, the publication of the Marine Industries Association of Palm Beach County.

> *The waterway was originally a private toll canal, the Florida Coast Line Canal and Transportation Company, founded by George Bradley, president of International Telephone and Telegraph. In 1881, he contracted with the state to build a waterway connecting the Matanzas River with the Indian River Lagoon. The idea was to provide the steamers working the Indian River with access to St. Augustine, then the southern terminus of the railroad. In 1882, the project expanded north to Jacksonville and south to Miami.*
>
> *By digging canals to connect natural lagoons, the company would create a waterway 50 feet wide and at least 5 feet deep at low water. In exchange, the state deeded 1,263 acres for every mile of waterway dredged. Before it was done in 1912, the state had turned over about a million acres—some 1,500 square miles.*
>
> *The work cost the private company about $3.5 million; it recouped $1.4 million from selling off some of the land it had received. Tolls were charged by stretching a chain across narrower sections. They were based on the amount of cargo or passengers.*

But, Roach explains, tolls were too meager, and when Henry Flagler's railroad was extended to West Palm Beach and eventually to Miami, the waterway, as an artery of commerce, fell into disuse and disrepair, defaulted on its bonds and went bankrupt.

Enter Harry Kelsey, the New England restaurateur and founder of Kelsey City. Kelsey eventually fell into financial ruin, and his planned utopian community eventually became Lake Park. Kelsey bought the waterway, seeing it as a way to attract potential land buyers.

In the boom years of the 1920s, the railroad, which by then had a monopoly on transportation, was charging what the market would bear, and the market demanded a cheaper alternative. Local governments reportedly were pressing Washington to privatize a public inland waterway.

The turning point came in 1921. Vacationing president-elect Warren G. Harding was on a schooner, heading for a golf outing, when the boat ran aground in the channel near Fort Lauderdale. He was stranded with his party for hours. Later, as president, he did not forget his unpleasant day in Florida.

President Harding called for a federal waterway project. A lengthy 1926 report by the U.S. Army Corps of Engineers concluded that improving the waterway would save the nation $400,000 to $1.6 million a year in transportation costs. The report called for building the waterway all the way from New England to Key West, making it seventy-five feet wide and eight feet deep. It projected a construction cost for the Florida part of $4.22 million, followed by $125,000 a year for maintenance.

In the deal, the original private waterway would be turned over to the feds, and local governments would provide areas to deposit dredged materials. In 1927, the state legislature created the Florida Inland Navigation District (FIND) to meet those conditions and authorized it to buy the original waterway for about $800,000 and hand it over to the feds.

According to Roach's history, the waterway was open and operating by 1935. Today, the Army Corps and FIND keep it at 12 feet deep and 125 feet wide from the Georgia border to Fort Pierce, then 10 feet deep and 124 feet wide down to Miami and, finally, 7 feet deep and 75 feet wide down to Crossbank, near Islamorada in the Florida Keys. The final stretch, down to Key West, was never finished.

For more information, contact the Florida Inland Navigation District at (561) 627-3386 or visit their website at www.aicw.org.

Originally published in the *Palm Beach Post*, December 3, 10 and 17, 2003.

The Okeechobee Waterway

Q: What is the Okeechobee Waterway?
A: Stretching across the state and through Lake Okeechobee, the 152-mile Okeechobee Waterway extends to the Gulf of Mexico near Fort Myers, via the Caloosahatchee, and to the Atlantic Ocean at Stuart, via the St. Lucie Canal.

In 1881, Hamilton Disston of Philadelphia, whose family had made its fortune selling Disston saws, bought four million acres of land in Central Florida, accounting for about 11 percent of the state's total land area. He paid $1 million. That's a remarkable twenty-five cents an acre.

Disston wanted to drain the land to create rich farm fields. But he also wanted to create waterways that would not only move products from the lake to the coast but also draw fishermen, pleasure boaters and tourists.

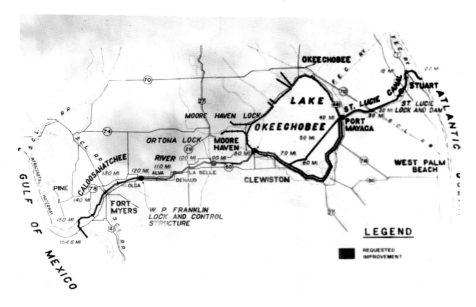

A map of the Okeechobee Waterway. Palm Beach Post *archives*.

One of his first projects was to carve the Caloosahatchee Canal, bridging the three-mile gap from where the Caloosahatchee River dead-ended into Lake Okeechobee. The *New Orleans Times Democrat* financed a group of explorers who sailed down the Kissimmee River, into Lake Okeechobee, through the canal and into the Caloosahatchee and down to Fort Myers. The November 1882 trek of nearly five hundred miles took fourteen days. The public was captivated.

On the other coast, the Everglades Drainage District carved the St. Lucie Canal between 1916 and 1928. It connected the lake to the eastern coast.

The Okeechobee Waterway was officially opened in Stuart on March 23, 1937, by a boat-a-cade that had left Fort Myers the previous day.

For U.S. Army Corps of Engineers Okeechobee Waterway information see the website www.saj.usace.army.mil/recreation.

Originally published in the *Palm Beach Post*, December 29, 2004.

The Collapse of the Royal Park Bridge

Q: Is it true that one of the bridges from West Palm Beach to Palm Beach collapsed once?
A: Yes. It was the Royal Park Bridge, the "middle bridge" of the three.

It happened on December 29, 1921. Here is the tale, according to Judge James R. Knott's "Brown Wrapper" historical series in the *Palm Beach Post*.

A new masonry structure was being built to replace the old wooden bridge, which had stood for about nine years. It was two days from being dedicated.

Sara Dean, wife of S. Bobo Dean, publisher of the *Palm Beach Daily News* ("The Shiny Sheet") rode her bicycle across at 10:00 a.m. She was apparently the only resident ever to use the doomed bridge.

About 2:00 p.m., as a steamroller was packing the surface, the head of construction heard a cracking noise and ordered the machine off. He and an assistant raced onto a barge to investigate from the waterline, but as soon as they did, a pier on the Palm Beach side gave way and the two spans crashed down, throwing workmen on the spans and the boat into the water.

Everyone was rescued, but later another span and another pier fell in. The bridge that inspectors had passed two days earlier was now a jumble of concrete chunks and steel rods. A civic uproar followed, with people calling for penalties for those responsible.

The Florida East Coast Railway Bridge from West Palm Beach to Palm Beach, December 18, 1921. *Historical Society of Palm Beach County.*

A temporary wooden structure was built, and it would be nearly two years before the bridge finally opened on August 11, 1924. A suit against the construction company ended in a settlement.

In 1958–59, the bridge was renovated, widened to four lanes and switched from a swing opening to a lift span.

A $50 million renovation took place in 2004.

For more information, contact the Historical Society of Palm Beach County at (561) 832-4164.

Originally published in the *Palm Beach Post*, April 14, 2004.

First to Die in the Line of Duty

Q: Who was the first law enforcement officer killed in the line of duty in Palm Beach County?
A: For years, it was believed to be Frederick Baker, a sheriff's deputy shot during a raid
on the Ashley gang, which terrorized South Florida in the 1910s and 1920s.

In February 1924, a posse led by Palm Beach County sheriff Bob Baker opened up on the Ashley camp in western Martin County. Joe Ashley, John's father, was shot as he tied his shoes. John, seeing his father hit, killed deputy

Palm Beach Police officer Joseph Smith, killed by poachers. Palm Beach Post *archives*.

Fred Baker. The gang fled; angry townspeople burned the Ashleys' camp and homes.

Nine months later, Ashley and three partners were shot dead on a bridge north of Fort Pierce. A judge accepted deputies' statements that the gangsters were trying to escape, but decades later, one of those deputies admitted that the criminals had been handcuffed when they were shot.

Fred Baker's status was unchanged until 1996, when Florida International University professor William Wilbanks unearthed the story of George Clem Douglas, killed on August 17, 1921, while trying to arrest a thief in Bare Beach, near Belle Glade.

Later in 1996, in a public ceremony seventy-five years after the fact, authorities added Douglas's name to the county's Fallen Deputy Memorial in West Palm Beach and submitted it for the National Law Enforcement Memorial in Washington. Douglas became one of nine county deputies believed to have been killed in the line of duty since the county and its sheriff's office were formed in 1909.

Douglas, a farmer, was talked into taking the job by town councils in the settlements of Bare Beach and Ritta, now ghost towns along the big lake. He held it for only five weeks before being shot, allegedly by Sam Wells, a 50-year-old laborer on a crew building the Miami Lake, where the Miami Canal meets Lake Okeechobee. Wells had been accused of cheating another man out of his paycheck during a card game. Wells was never arrested in the slaying.

For more information, contact the Historical Society of Palm Beach County at (561) 832-4164.

Originally published in the *Palm Beach Post*, August 9, 2000.

Lynching in Florida

Lynching: it's one of the ugliest words in our lexicon. Florida is the most assimilated of the southern states. But from 1882 to 1930, a higher percentage of blacks—79.8 per 100,000—were lynched here than in any other state.

One such outrage occurred in 1926 in Delray Beach. The *Palm Beach Post* reported the incident a month later; it was not a locally written story but one from the Associated Press:

Sam Nelson, alias Joseph Johnson, negro, was taken from the jail at Delray and lynched near that city by unidentified persons on September 26, according to reports from reliable sources reaching here tonight.

No official announcement of the incident has been made, although a coroner's jury was said to have investigated the affair and to have rendered a verdict that Nelson suffered "death at the hands of parties unknown."

The negro was said to have been charged with attempted criminal assault on a white woman in Miami. On the afternoon of September 26, he was arrested by authorities in Delray, 60 miles north. The following morning the steel door of the jail was found battered open, and the negro gone. A short time later the body of Nelson, riddled with bullets, was found on the bank of a canal near the military trail, four miles west of Delray.

Delray Beach Historical Society's Dottie Patterson found the following in the city council's September 26 minutes for that year:

Mr. W.M. Croft, Chief of Police, reported verbally in regard to the removal of a colored prisoner from jail by forceable entry into the jail on the night of September 26 or the early morning of Sept. 27…that he had refused to turn said prisoner over to a man who purported to be from Miami.

Originally published in the *Palm Beach Post*, September 25, 2008.

A Boathouse Built with Green Stamps

I live in the old boathouse in the back of Suni Sands Mobile Home Park, which was originally built in the early 1900s by S&H Green Stamp co-founder Thomas Sperry. His estate overlooked the Jupiter Inlet, and the boathouse was built as both a ballroom and, of course, as a house for his boats. I am extremely interested in any information you may know of or any old photos that may exist concerning the boathouse.

—Tom Saunders, Jupiter

The mobile home park is on the site of Sperry's winter estate on the inlet. He bought the property in 1904 and enlarged and remodeled the home, building a sea wall and boathouse.

One historical source suggests that the boathouse was already there when Sperry bought the estate, while another says that it was built in 1906, according to Michael Zaidman, curator of the Loxahatchee River Historical

"Uncle Joe" and his friend William Sperry with the day's catch, circa 1925. *Loxahatchee River Historical Society.*

Society. In any event, the boathouse's upstairs was a ballroom with a scenic view of the Loxahatchee River.

The property was sold in 1925, and William Sperry died two years later. After the boom busted, it was returned to Sperry's widow. The mobile home park was sold to private owners in the late 1940s.

Mrs. Sperry died in 1955. Sperry's home was torn down, and the boathouse was later converted to apartments. The current owners have had the property since 1976, manager Steven J. Burns said in 2003. He said that the park owners might renovate the boathouse.

Burt Reynolds filmed part of an episode of his 1980s detective drama *B.L. Stryker* at the boathouse, and the British Broadcasting Corporation, for a murder-mystery feature, filmed a fight and shootout at the boathouse and a chase through the park.

For more information, contact the Loxahatchee River Historical Society at (561) 747-6639 or visit their website at www.lrhs.org

Originally published in the *Palm Beach Post,* January 8, 2003.

The Pennocks

We have seen pictures (probably taken in the early 1900s) of the Pennock Plantation in Jupiter. Was Pennock Lane (between Toney Penna Drive and Center Street) named for the family and could you find out where the Pennock Plantation was located?

—Earl and Patty Miller, Jupiter

The old plantation dates back to the start of the twentieth century, when Abraham L. Pennock, a Philadelphia florist who tired of the expense of hot houses, recalled visits to South Florida. He sent two sons to scout a place to raise asparagus plumosus, a popular plant often considered a fern, although it is in a different plant category.

Son Henry set up an operation, locating the plantation around the area of what is now Pennock Lane. Soon, Jupiter was a center of fern farming, with as many as seventeen facilities. Farms also thrived in the Boynton Beach–Hypoluxo area.

For decades, the Pennocks had more than seven acres of ferns growing under shelters, but by the mid-1950s, the market had softened and the Pennocks were growing on only an acre and a half. Pennock also operated a large dairy and was one of the largest employers in the northern part of the county.

The plantation's remaining buildings were destroyed in a 1970 fire.

In the late 1920s, Pennock and some other businesses and residents became disenchanted with Jupiter's government and taxes and decided to take drastic action. Soon, they had their own town. For three decades, it was a municipality, even though it had no government or services. People couldn't even agree on its name, sometimes calling it "Plumosa City."

The six-square-mile town in and around Pennock Lane was incorporated in 1929 and again in 1930. According to *Five Thousand Years on the Loxahatchee*, by James Snyder, and articles in 2000 in the *Jupiter Courier*, the city was operated from the offices of the Pennock Plantation. The town was officially incorporated on July 25, 1929, and began holding monthly meetings, usually to say that there was no business to address and adjourning. For some reason, the town was again incorporated on May 22, 1930. The 1935 census showed thirty-seven residents.

During a development spat in the mid-1950s, parties argued whether the town existed. In 1957, developer Raymond E. Olson made plans to create the 268-lot neighborhood of Eastview Manor, an area between Center Street and Indiantown Road. After failing to meet county requirements, Olson got approval from Plumosus City. But residents called the county commission to say that the town existed on paper only. After the commission gave tentative approval, Olson built some homes, sold a few of them and eventually went bankrupt. By March 1959, residents asked the legislature to formally dissolve the municipality, which it did on June 18, 1959.

For more information, contact the Loxahatchee River Historical Society at (561) 747-6639 or visit their website at www.lrhs.org

Originally published in the *Palm Beach Post*, June 2 and 9, 2004.

Jupiter's Early Lawmen

There is a section of Alternate A1A from Donald Ross to Riverside Drive that is called the Glynn Mayo Highway. I read somewhere that he had been a police chief in Jupiter. What did he do that a highway was named for him?

—Regina Brazinskas, Tequesta

In April 1992, the stretch of Alternate A1A—State Road 811—from Donald Ross Road north to where it meets U.S. 1 and State Road 707 in Jupiter was named Glynn Mayo Highway. It honors Mayo, who died of cancer at age sixty-two in May 1991. He was Jupiter's police chief and ran the department for twenty-eight years.

In his obituary, friends described him as a Dennis Weaver lookalike who talked with a southern drawl and handled his job with a homey, Andy-of-Mayberry demeanor. The son of a school bus driver and a gas station owner, he was named a constable for the northern part of the county in 1955 and became police chief three years later.

Captain James Woodard, who became Mayo's first part-time officer in 1961, said that up to that time, the telephone at his desk also rang at his bedside.

By the time Mayo retired in 1986, he was managing a department with thirty-seven sworn officers and a $1.75 million budget.

My 2001 column on Glynn Mayo brought a response from Byron Wakefield of Jupiter. Several articles during the years have said that Mayo, who died in 1991, was named a constable in North County in 1955 and became the city's first chief three years later. But Wakefield says that the first chief was James E. Williams Sr., in 1926, a year after Jupiter was incorporated on February 9, 1925.

Wakefield cites *Loxahatchee Lament*, a collection of early settlers' memoirs assembled by the *Jupiter Courier* in 1974. In it, Williams's widow is quoted as saying that he was the first chief, serving for three years before switching to the Palm Beach Police. An accompanying July 15, 1926 photograph identifies Williams as the police chief.

A 2000 article in the *Courier* identified Williams as holding office in March 1928. It says that Mayor Charles Bennet wrote to the town commission, accusing Williams and Vice Mayor R.C. Albertson of pocketing liquor confiscated from a bootlegger.

Bennet wanted Williams fired and Albertson booted from office. The article says that it is not known what came of Williams but that he later worked for the Palm Beach County Sheriff's Office, not the Palm Beach Police.

Jupiter city clerk Sally Boylan says that there's nothing in town minutes or other records to confirm this. But Carlin White says that it was Williams. White, born in 1907, served as the town's mayor from 1970 to 1976. He was a young man in Jupiter in 1926 and remembers Williams as chief. We will go with Mr. Carlin, who was ninety-seven in 2003; he was there.

Originally published in the *Palm Beach Post,* July 18, 2001, and March 26, 2003.

Bill Boutwell: The Inventor of Half-and-Half

Could you please tell me the origin of Boutwell Road in Lake Worth? Since I have the same last name, people are always asking me if it's my road.

—Jeff Boutwell, Lake Worth

William A. Boutwell was a longtime dairyman who was born in Vermont and educated in Ontario. He came to the area from Massachusetts in the 1920s with his wife and four children. He opened a grocery store and masonry supply business and, in 1927, started a dairy herd on five acres in what is now Palm Springs.

Boutwell, who is credited with creating the process that produces half-and-half, started with seventy-five customers and one hundred head of cattle. He retired in 1956, and the family sold the business in 1965; by then it had eleven hundred cattle and was one of Florida's leading dairies.

Boutwell also served on the city commission from 1924 to 1927, including a stint as vice mayor, which then included the duties of city administrator. He also served on the Palm Beach County School Board and was the first president of the Lake Worth Lions Club.

He bought some land in Lake Worth, and today's Boutwell Road, between Lake Worth Road and Tenth Avenue, is in that area.

Boutwell died at age ninety-eight in June 1982.

For more information, contact the Museum of the City of Lake Worth at (561) 586-1700.

Originally published in the *Palm Beach Post*, December 5, 2001.

South Florida's Female Mayors: Lantana, Moore Haven

Jack Carpenter, a former Lantana Town Council member and president of the Lantana Historical Society, has offered the fascinating tidbit that the town's first mayor was a woman. Carpenter cites Mary Linehan's *Early Lantana, Her Neighbors and More*.

On July 20, 1921, when the town incorporated, J.H. Vance was elected mayor. But he changed his mind right after the election and never took office; one story said that he found out he lived outside town limits. So the town appointed Ellen M. Anderson, who served for two years. Women had held the right to vote for less than a year, since August 26, 1920.

Anderson was followed by another woman, Mary S. Paddock, who served until 1924. Carpenter says that officials of a state agency called him a few years ago saying they believed Anderson was the state's first female mayor, so that's what he's said ever since, in his lectures.

On June 8, 1917, Moore Haven incorporated on the west side of Lake Okeechobee. Marian Horwitz was elected its first mayor, three years before women's suffrage. She is believed to be the first female mayor in Florida and the South and one of the first in the country.

"I'm going to have to change my speech," Carpenter lamented.

Originally published in the *Palm Beach Post*, September 1, 2004.

Pearl City

As Addison Mizner spread pink across the horizon, as the glitterati made Boca Raton a tropical paradise, people lived, raised families and died in a modest three-block area called Pearl City.

Florida Atlantic University professors Arthur S. Evans and David Lee are authors of the 1990 oral history *Pearl City, Florida: A Black Community Remembers*. Evans interviewed twenty-six elderly pioneers of Pearl City, and he and Lee researched and wrote the book.

Pearl City was formed in 1915, a decade before Boca Raton was incorporated and the Boca Raton Resort and Club opened. The original settlers worked on the large, white-owned farms in the area or operated small subsistence farms.

Eventually, the small black community spread beyond the original three-block area near Federal Highway and Glades Road to include about another eight blocks to the north.

When the Mizner Park shopping and entertainment complex caused downtown property values to skyrocket in the 1990s, the value of Pearl City's homes rose as well.

"Living in Pearl City was all right," said Q.J. "Bud" Jackson, one of the pioneers interviewed for the book. "That's all we knew anyway. We lived in what you called 'colored town.' That's all there was. We were used to that."

Jackson, a landscaping supervisor for the city for twenty-eight years before he retired, was brought to Boca Raton from the Florida Panhandle as an infant in 1925. His home was demolished in the great 1928 hurricane, and the family moved into Pearl City about 1936; his father bought three lots for seventy-five dollars each.

About a year later, Jackson was only twelve or thirteen when he got a job operating a new-fangled automatic dishwashing machine at the Boca Raton Resort and Club.

Originally published in the *Palm Beach Post*, January 16, 2000.

How Hillsboro Became Belle Glade

Q: How did Belle Glade get its name?

A: Actually, this story has become quite an issue. The town, settled in 1917 along Lake Okeechobee at the Hillsboro Canal and a central location for smaller settlements along Lake Okeechobee, was originally called Hillsboro. The story behind its name has always been that a blackboard was set up in the town's only hotel, and guests and residents were invited to suggest a new town name, with the winner being a derivation of "Belle of the Glades."

But Frank Stallings, at the time ninety-three and living in Central Florida in the Lake County town of Tavares, offered a different version in 2001.

Stallings's family was the fourth to move to the settlement now known as Belle Glade. The town got its post office in 1917 and was incorporated on April 9, 1928, five months before the great Okeechobee hurricane.

Stallings said that various businessmen who had helped found the town gathered every week or two to discuss farming and other topics. At one meeting, in the fall of 1921, the issue of the town's name came up for consideration. Warren Badger, the postmaster, suggested Badger. Walter Greer, on tap to be mayor, suggested Greer. Both were voted down.

Then up stood Captain Stone, skipper of the boat that for six years was the settlement's only link to civilization, plying the New River Canal to Fort Lauderdale. He suggested that the town be named for his boat, the *Glade Bell*. Stallings, who would have been a teenager at the time, says that he was at that meeting and made a suggestion.

"I said, 'Captain Stone: Why don't you turn it around and call it Belle Glade?' It was almost unanimous," Stallings recalled.

Records show that a post office was established on March 31, 1917, at Torry Island and was replaced by the Belle Glade office on March 29, 1921, which is earlier than the fall of 1921 but pretty close.

Joseph Orsenigo, a leading Glades historian and member of the Belle Glade Museum Board, said in an October 16, 2001 note that "the hotel/ blackboard scenario is ahead 2 to 1."

Originally published in the *Palm Beach Post*, November 21, 2001.

Mizner's Monkey

Q: Are there any cemeteries in Palm Beach?
A: Only one, but not for people. Two small plots in Via Mizner, the first shopping
*   arcade built on Worth Avenue, bear the remains of a family dog and a very*
*   famous spider monkey.*

Little Johnnie Brown was the pet of Addison Mizner, the famed Palm Beach architect and Boca Raton developer. Mizner loved to shoulder Johnnie and another monkey, Deuteronomy, and even hand-stitched a silk-lined sombrero, with a chin strap, for Johnnie.

In 1925, Mizner's monkeys were invited to the "Monkey Trial" in Tennessee, where a high school teacher was criminally charged for teaching evolution. Mizner declined. He and his pets were forced out of their residence at the exclusive Everglades Club, which he had designed, after he and the

Developer Addison Mizner with a parrot and his beloved pet monkey, Johnnie Brown. Palm Beach Post *archives*.

club's president argued over money and the president banned animals from the apartments.

Mizner survived Johnnie by only six years. The animal's marker reads: "Johnnie Brown. The Human Monkey. Died April 30, 1927."

Beside Johnnie's plot is a grave for Rose Sachs's dog, Laddie. Sachs and her husband, Morton, bought Mizner's villa and lived there for forty-seven years. When she wanted to bury her dog next to Johnnie, the town permitted it, but she had to have Laddie cremated first. The dog's marker reads, "Our Laddie 1949–1959."

A gift shop at 347 Worth Avenue is called Johnnie Brown's to honor the nearby grave. And there is one other homage to pets: a special dog trough in front of Phillips Galleries at 318 Worth Avenue was designed by well-known architect John Volk in honor of his schnauzer, Hans.

Originally published in the *Palm Beach Post*, November 2, 2005.

A decorated car in a parade for the Seminole Sun Dance, precursor to the modern-day SunFest music festival. *Jan Davidson Collection.*

George Wright: Wright Field

After Municipal Athletic Field was built in 1924, why was it renamed Wright Field in 1927?

—Bill Butler, suburban West Palm Beach

The ballpark—renamed Connie Mack Field in 1952 and now the parking garage for the Kravis Center for the Performing Arts—might be long gone, but it still sparks memories. The "Wright" is George L. Wright, city manager in the 1920s and the man behind the stadium.

According to an article about the dedication on December 18, 1924, it appeared that the opening would be delayed for a month, but Wright pushed contractors to rush it to completion, and the season's first game was "played on grounds which are said to be second to none in the South." The city knows only that Wright died in 1926; the field was named for him the following year.

Possible relatives were tracked down in Virginia but weren't related after all. Readers: can you help? One insight comes from this anecdote, provided years later by the late, great Palm Beach County commissioner Lake Lytal: Sometime in the 1920s, Palm Beach High School's football team was playing at Fort Lauderdale High School. Wright's son, Edloe, was center on the Palm Beach High team. Wright got into a sideline hassle for what he perceived as unfair officiating—and was arrested!

Additional facts about Wright Field/Connie Mack from past columns include: grandstands held about two thousand spectators; black fans watched from a small section in the right-field corner; and the total capacity was about thirty-five hundred.

The field became dormant in 1962 when the municipal stadium was built. It was bulldozed in 1992 to make room for a garage for the new Kravis Center.

Originally published in the *Palm Beach Post*, March 26, 2009.

Banned in Boca

Good news: it is not a crime to be a bum. When then city attorney Frank Bartolone visited schools and other groups in the mid-1990s, he enjoyed displaying the city's 1929 code of ordinances, written three years after incorporation.

"I show it as part of how regulations have evolved over the years," Bartolone said in 1995. "Now, regulations like that have to stand more strict scrutiny."

In the stilted language of the period, the code outlaws vagrancy in no uncertain terms:

> *That all rogues, and vagabonds; idle and dissolute persons; tramps who go about begging; persons who use juggling or unlawful games of play; common pipers or fiddlers; stubborn children; runaways; common drunkards; common night walkers; thieves, pilferers, lewd, wanton and lascivious persons in speech or behavior; common railers and brawlers; people*

Boca Raton Fire Department, August 27, 1927. The fire truck was housed in a garage at the Boca Raton city hall, now the city's historical museum. *Boca Raton Historical Society.*

who neglect their calling or employment, or who have no visible means of support, and those who do not provide for themselves or their families; and all other idle and disorderly persons shall be considered vagrants and upon conviction of vagrancy shall be fined not exceeding one hundred dollars ($100.00) or imprisonment not exceeding thirty (30) days, or both.

Said Bartolone, "I especially like the part about stubborn children."

The city's voluminous code was gutted in the early 1990s to delete laws that were archaic, redundant to state law or no match for the U.S. Constitution.

"We got rid of probably half our code," said Steve Melnick, the city's code enforcement attorney. "It was so difficult to track ordinances."

A state statute on vagrancy was on the books for decades before it was declared unconstitutional by the U.S. Supreme Court about 1980, said Ray Marky, a former assistant attorney general and an unofficial historian of state law.

Originally published in the *Palm Beach Post*, November 24, 1995.

III

Palm Beach Past

THE BUST

The WPA

One of my most treasured, and worn, Florida books is *The WPA Guide to Florida*. Under the Federal Writers Project, part of President Franklin Roosevelt's Works Progress Administration, writers went down country roads gathering documents and taking down the tales of folks who would tell them.

In the case of *The WPA Guide to Florida*, originally called *Florida: Guide to the Southernmost State* when it was published in 1939, what resulted is a remarkable snapshot. It portrays a Florida still in the Depression and yet to be rescued by World War II and the infusion of federal money. It was a sleepy place, with only about one million souls from Key West to Pensacola, unrecognizable from today's crowded, heavily developed behemoth of millions.

The following are some interesting excerpts from the *Guide* (populations in brackets are 2002 estimates):

About northern Palm Beach County the *Guide* said:

> *Jupiter: Population: 176* [42,296]...*A small trading community.*

> *Riviera: Population: 811* [31,077]...*Here lives a colony of Conchs, so named for the variety of shellfish they eat...Many are descendants of English fishermen who, during and after the* [First] *World War, left the Bahamas and settled on Singer's Island, opposite Riviera. The Conchs left their island settlement and removed to the mainland here during the 1920s, when a "land shark" extravagantly raised rents on Singer's Island.*
> [Riviera changed to Riviera Beach in 1941.]

About central Palm Beach County, the *Guide* noted:

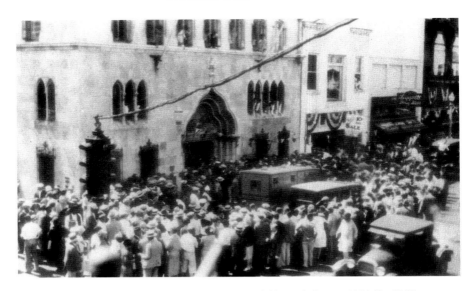

The run on the Farmers Bank at Olive Avenue and Clematis Street, 1926. By 1933, more than two hundred Florida banks had closed and the Great Depression was well under way. Palm Beach Post *archives*.

West Palm Beach: Population: 26,610 [86,194]*…Although it is the business and railroad center for Palm Beach, on the opposite shore, West Palm Beach, with its large hotels and recreational facilities, is a popular winter resort in its own right…Bicycles are a popular means of conveyance, but in the closely built-up business area, motorcar congestion has necessitated extensive one-way traffic regulations…Curio shops display articles fashioned locally of native woods, grasses, shells and clays.*

Lake Worth: Population: 5,940 [35,292]*…Municipal golf course greens fee: 75 cents…A tourist town of many bright-colored stucco residences…A municipally owned casino (bathhouses) faces the ocean. Revenue from municipally owned ice, cold-storage, electric-light, and water plants pay almost all of the town's operating expenses…An ostrich and alligator farm (admission 25 cents) has alligators of all ages, ranging from babies just hatched to a battle-scarred veteran estimated to be 400 years old. Ostriches, crocodiles, monkeys, lemurs, kangaroos, and snakes are also to be seen.*

Lantana: Population: 811 [9,477].

Hypoluxo: Population: 43 [2,420].

Palm Beach Past: The Bust

About southern Palm Beach County, then almost all farmland and scattered resorts, the *Guide* said:

> *Boynton: Population: 1,121* [62,847]...*On a sandy ridge in an area of rich farmland extending westward to the Everglades. Many Finnish farmers have settled here. Left from Boynton 1 mile on State 195 across the Intracoastal Waterway to Boynton Beach (bathhouses, casino, refreshment stand).* [Boynton Beach split from Boynton in 1931. In 1937, it changed to Ocean Ridge and Boynton was renamed Boynton Beach.]

> *Gulf Stream, a small settlement, clusters about the wealthy Gulf Stream Club (private) and its 18-hole golf course.*

> *Delray Beach: Population: 1,053* [61,527]...*Delray Country Club and Golf Course greens fees: 50 cents.* [The town], *settled in 1901, is a tourist resort and the center of an area producing beans, peppers, tomatoes, sugar cane, and citrus fruit. Many Michigan farmers of German ancestry have bought farms in the vicinity...Left from Delray Beach on Ocean Boulevard to Sunken Gardens (admission 35 cents). Exhibiting such curiosities as the dainty lipstick flower, the silk-cotton tree, the pelican flower, and the jack-knife tree, bearing fruit often 40 pounds in weight.*

> *Boca Raton: Population: 447* [75,580]...*On the landscaped waterfront is the Boca Raton Club, (private), approached by a wide driveway planted by royal and coconut palms, crotons, bougainvilleas, hibiscus, and oleanders. Originally designed as a hotel by Addison Mizner, it is an excellent example of Spanish-Gothic architecture treated in the Mizner manner.*

The following is an excerpt about Palm Beach:

> *Population: 1,707* [9,674]...*Taxi from Morrison Field* [now Palm Beach International Airport]: *50 cents. Ferry to West Palm Beach: 5 cents. Movie theaters: two, open winter only. Golf: Palm Beach Country Club, greens fee $2.50...*
>
> *Worth Avenue, at the widest part of the island and the southern extremity of the shopping district, is a four-block street of smart shops, including branches of metropolitan stores....North and south of this area are rich estates surrounded by vine-cloaked walls raised high to ensure seclusion.*

The restrained magnificence of these properties is the result of lavish expenditures, expert landscaping, and continuous care...

Palm Beach is regarded as the winter counterpart of Newport—cosmopolitan, individual, and independent. Its habitues constitute a fragment of international society seeking June in January and the pleasures afforded by right of social prestige and heavy purse...A vanguard of servants descends from the North in December to set the stage. With the new year, private railroad cars are parked on West Palm Beach sidings and sumptuous houseboats and yachts from distant ports moor in the sheltered waters of Lake Worth...

Palm Beach has no Negro settlement, and Negroes are not allowed on the streets after dark unless actively employed in the city.

The following excerpt refers to the Glades area. Again, note the fascination with race:

Belle Glade: Population: 1,646 [14,869]...A municipal ordinance requires that all Negroes, except those employed within the town, be off the streets by 10:30 p.m. On Saturdays they are permitted to remain in the business district until midnight. The fertility of the soil in the region is reflected in the Negro story of two boys who were planting corn one morning and discovered that it was sprouting immediately behind them...

Pahokee: Population: 2,256 [6,078]...From Christmas to April, Pahokee is a 24-hour town; long trains of refrigerated cars roll out for northern markets day and night; the streets are noisy and crowded; bars, restaurants and gambling places are seldom closed...Itinerant pickers, both white and Negro, known as "traveling hands," swarm into this region at harvest time, as into other fruit and vegetable growing districts of the state, occupying tents, rows of tumbledown cottages, and ramshackle boarding houses.

South Bay: Population: 235 [3,934]...A Negro worker who passed unscathed through several hurricanes has graphically described the velocity of a tropical gale: "One day the wind blowed so hard, it blowed a well up out of the ground; blowed so hard, it blowed a crooked road straight. Another time it blowed an' blowed, an' scattered the days of the week, so bad that Sunday didn't come till late Tuesday mo'nin.'"

Palm Beach Past: The Bust

I've told you about U.S. 1 in Palm Beach County and a little about the story of the U.S. highway system, which was the only way to travel before the interstates. What follows is some more history.

Many federal highways were mutations of original roads, even horse paths. In the first few decades of the twentieth century, when motor travel was in its adolescence, the train was still king. By the mid-1920s, associations had unilaterally given names to more than 250 routes. But the number of registered vehicles had gone from fewer than 500,000 in 1910 to nearly 10 million in 1920. More than 26 million would be registered by 1930. So the numbered system was adopted in 1926.

For the most part, U.S. highways radiate from the northeastern United States. East–west roads have even numbers; north–south ones, odd numbers. Thus, the Florida Panhandle has the high-numbered U.S. 90, and the road heading down the East Coast, from the top of Maine to Key West, is U.S. 1.

According to the 1939 *Federal Writers' Project WPA Guide to Florida*:

> *U.S. 1 becomes a veritable Midway, with innumerable signs and loudspeakers ballyhooing sights and sites, amusements, foods, patent medicines, trailer camps, and roadside cabins ranging from one-room frame shacks to elaborate two-and three-room stucco dwellings. Souvenir stands offer carved coconuts, seashells, honey, guava jelly, and miscellany of bewildering edibles and mementoes; nurseries exhibit subtropical plants for sales; deep-sea fishing camps, Indian villages, and tropical gardens are blatantly advertised.*

The more things change, the more they stay the same.

For more information contact the Historical Society of Palm Beach County at (561) 832-4164; the Museum of the City of Lake Worth at (561) 586-1700; the Loxahatchee River Historical Society at (561) 747-6639 or visit their website at www.lrhs.org; the Boynton Beach Historical Society at Box 12, Boynton Beach 33435; the Delray Beach Historical Society at (561) 274-9578; the Henry Morrison Flagler Museum at (561) 655-2833; or the Lawrence Will Museum at Palm Beach County Public Library, Belle Glade Branch at (561) 996-3453.

Originally published in the *Palm Beach Post*, November 27 and December 4, 11, 18 and 25, 2002.

The Campus Shop

When did the Campus Shop open up? I know it is in my mother's 1939 yearbook. Also, why was the band in that yearbook called the "Jay Cees" instead of the later PBHS Band?

—Jim Philips of Lexington, Kentucky, alumnus of Palm Beach High School

For answers, I went to the Palm Beach High oracle, ophthalmologist Dr. Reginald Stambaugh, founding chairman of the school's historical committee.

According to our archives, the shop at Georgia (now Sapodilla) and Hibiscus Streets opened in 1938. But Stambaugh, who died in December

The Campus Shop, which opened in the 1930s, was in its heyday during the war years. Palm Beach Post *archives.*

2007, said that the shop had already been open for several years when he was in grade school in 1935.

The shop was run by Crystal Eggert, whose husband, Johnnie, operated Johnnie's Playland, a magic and gag shop in the small building that is now the Palm Beach High Museum on Flagler Drive.

Crystal and her sister, Marie Carlson, sold school supplies, sandwiches and drinks to kids who crossed the street after school—and sometimes during classes.

The Eggerts closed the place in 1969, not long after a racially motivated fight led to a stabbing. It reopened in November 1985 under new management but shut down again soon after that.

Johnnie Eggert died in the 1950s; Crystal, in 1993.

As for the "Jay Cees" band, with the Depression in full swing, Stambaugh said, the band needed money to travel and was sponsored by the Junior Chamber of Commerce.

For more information, visit the Palm Beach High School alumni group's website at www.pbhsalumni.org or contact the Palm Beach High School Historical Committee and Museum at (561) 835-1681.

Originally published in the *Palm Beach Post*, November 15, 2006.

Palm Beach Kennel Club

The Palm Beach Kennel Club opened its doors on February 17, 1932. The corner of Congress Avenue and Belvedere Road, across from Palm Beach International Airport in unincorporated West Palm Beach, is a busy place now. Back then, it was the hinterlands.

But four thousand people attended the opening—a pretty good turnout considering the county's population at the time was about fifty-two thousand, half of which lived in West Palm Beach. At the time, racing took place only at night and only during the winter "season."

Local sportsman O.M. Carmichael built the track. It went through two more owners. The third owner built a grandstand and increased fourfold the mutual handle, or the total wagered.

The track's modern history began in 1970 when it was sold to Art Rooney, patriarch of the Pittsburgh Steelers. Over the ensuing decades, Rooney and his five sons presided over five Steelers Super Bowl wins. Rooney died at age eighty-seven in August 1988.

The Palm Beach Kennel Club, shown here during a 1975 race, opened in 1932. *Historical Society of Palm Beach County*.

The biggest excitement in the three-eighths-mile-long track's history probably occurred on the night of June 4, 1994, when Pat C. Rendezvous won her thirty-third straight race, setting a world record. She went on to win three more before the streak ended.

Almost as famous was "Rusty," the oversized artificial bone, attached to a rod, that moved around the track, tempting the hounds. Dogs had originally chased a rabbit by the same name. Humanity prevailed, but the name carried over. The name comes from the squeaks that emanate from the moving bone. A 1980 contest renamed the bone "wishbone," but that didn't stick.

When the track celebrated its fiftieth birthday in 1982, it found patrons who had attended on opening night and made them guests of honor.

In recent years, competition from American Indian casinos and the state lottery have cut into the Kennel Club's success. In 1991, the state approved year-round racing, betting on television broadcasts from other dog, horse and jai alai venues, as well as in-house card games.

For more information, visit the Palm Beach Kennel Club's website at www.pbkennelclub.com.

Originally published in the *Palm Beach Post*, February 14, 2007.

A Learning Oasis: The Whites

George and Emma White knew the key to success for blacks in turn-of-the-century Florida: education. The Whites had an inviolate rule: everyone went to school, even if it meant going to West Palm Beach, North Florida or even Virginia. Fourteen of their sixteen children lived to adulthood, most got high school diplomas and eight went to college or professional or vocational schools. All twenty-one grandchildren attended college.

George, born in 1856 near Lake City, worked as a casket maker, carpenter and farmer in Alachua, near Gainesville, where he met Emma, born in 1878. The family farmed on fifteen acres obtained through the state's Homestead Act.

About 1919, a nursery businessman persuaded the Whites to come to Gomez, near what is now Hobe Sound in southern Martin County. George worked in his spare time to build a six-bedroom, two-story home at 613 East Church Street in Stuart. The Whites moved there in 1922.

After George White died in 1933, the home was a haven for black people who couldn't otherwise find lodging in the days of segregation. There were

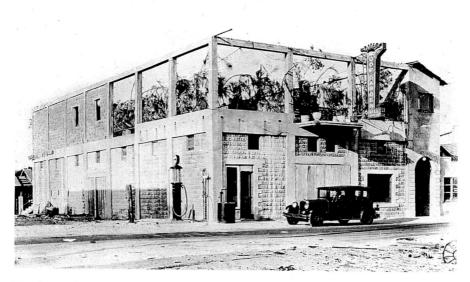

The Sunset Cocktail Lounge drew the biggest black acts to West Palm Beach starting in the 1930s. Palm Beach Post *archives*.

church leaders, teachers new to the area or students who came to Stuart for games or practices and finished too late to catch the last bus.

Emma White died in 1967 at the age of eighty-nine. In 1995, Martin County Black Heritage began a push to renovate the home and make it the county's first black cultural and history center. However, city inspectors said that it would cost too much to make the structure safe, so it remained abandoned.

Originally published in the *Palm Beach Post*, March 24, 2004.

Bean City

Driving from West Palm Beach to Fort Myers on State Road 80, we used to pass through "Bean City" in western Palm Beach County. Whatever happened to it?
—Rodney Dillon, co-owner, Past Perfect Florida History Bookstore

According to Glades historian Joseph Orsenigo and a 1978 *Miami Herald* article, Bean City got its name from the late Arthur Wells, the twenty-nine-year-old son of a Daytona Beach orange grower who hopped a boat from

Fort Lauderdale to the Glades in 1913. Wells, who was also mayor of Belle Glade from 1937 to 1939, planted string beans on a half acre and got other settlers to help him harvest the beans, which he sent by barge to the coast and eventually to New York. It marked the first time winter beans were available in that region, and they sold for an unheard-of thirteen dollars a hamper. Folks up there started talking about Bean City.

Wells later expanded to hundreds of acres and built a Baptist church and homes for laborers. The 1928 hurricane blew away the entire town and killed many workers and farm animals. Within two years, Wells had rebuilt. There was a general store and a post office. A competitor of sorts, John Evans, arrived in 1939, and everyone in the town worked for either Wells or Evans, who eventually helped found South Bay Growers.

By the time Wells died in 1961, he had sold most of his land to sugar growers. The new State Road 80 had bypassed Bean City, and it was turning into a ghost town. Now, it is just a small settlement of perhaps one dozen residents about a mile west of South Bay.

Originally published in the *Palm Beach Post*, July 9, 2003.

Bacom Road, Pahokee

Can you tell us how Bacon Point Road got its name? (Pig farms, perhaps?) Also, what is the correct pronunciation of Pahokee?

—*JoAnn Baker, suburban West Palm Beach*

Actually, it is Bacom Point Road, not Bacon, and it is named for William Bacom, according to his grandson, Charles A. Bacom Jr. of Port Orange, near Daytona Beach. He said that the family name traces back to Ireland.

"I'm the oldest Bacom there is," Charles, then eighty-three, said in 2004. Charles said that William came from Ohio about the time of World War I and began a farming and catfish business on an actual point that jutted into Lake Okeechobee. William died of a heart attack in 1922 or 1923, his grandson said. By then, William's son, Charles Sr., had moved away from the area and was in the yachting business. Charles Jr. joined him in 1935, and Charles Sr. died in 1982.

After the 1928 hurricane, construction began on the giant dike. Parts of the lake were filled in, including Bacom Point. Now, the Pahokee airport, along Bacom Point Road, sits on what used to be the open lake west of Bacom Point, according to Charles Jr. Retired Pahokee Police chief Carmen

Salvatore III, whose grandfather, pioneer Carmen Salvatore, settled the area right after World War I, confirmed the details.

As for the pronunciation of Pahokee's name, it is "puh-HOE-kee." For the origin of Pahokee's name, we turn to no less an authority than environmental visionary Marjory Stoneman Douglas. In her most famous book, she describes the name that Native Americans gave to the Everglades: "Pa-hay-okee." The phrase translates to "grassy waters"—or, in the case of Douglas's classic volume, *River of Grass*.

Originally published in the *Palm Beach Post*, March 24, 2004.

The First Radio Station

Q: What was Palm Beach County's first radio station?
A: That would be the well-traveled WJNO. It signed on at 1:00 p.m. on July 31, 1936. Originally a CBS affiliate, it aired everything from classical music to Steve Allen.

WJNO survived the Depression, World War II and the advent of television and computers. WJNO-TV, Channel 5 (NBC), signed on August 22, 1954; it became WPTV in 1956 and was bought by Scripps-Howard in December 1961.

WJNO-AM has also moved across the dial a few times. Fairbanks Communications bought it in 1979; in 1997, it bought the station at 1040 AM and moved WJNO to that spot on the dial, after more than six decades at 1230, to take advantage of its strong signal strength in southern Palm Beach and Broward Counties.

Fairbanks sold WJNO in December 1999 to Texas-based Clear Channel Communications, which moved it to 1290 AM, switching with WBZT. That limited WJNO's nighttime signal from Boynton Beach south.

For more information, contact Clear Channel Communications at (561) 616-6600.

Originally published in the *Palm Beach Post*, March 29, 2000.

License Plates

Q: A long time ago, license plates had a number for each county instead of the county's name on the plate. What was the number for Palm Beach County?

A biplane flies over Palm Beach just after Morrison Field, later Palm Beach International Airport, was built in the 1930s. World War II and the resurgence of tourism and migration pulled South Florida out of the Great Depression. Palm Beach Post *archives*.

A: Starting in 1938, the state assigned each of its sixty-seven counties a number, based not on its population but on the amount of taxes collected on gasoline. Over the years, counties fluctuated in size, but the numbers were untouched until the state began spelling out county names on tags in 1975.

Dade (now Miami-Dade) was number 1. Palm Beach was 6. Nearby Martin was 42, St. Lucie 24 and Indian River 32. Okeechobee was 57, Broward 10 and Monroe (the Keys) was 38. A 90 was a duplicate. A 68 meant you got your tag at the state agency instead of a particular county.

All the way back in 1905, the state had required car owners to register their vehicles and issued paper certificates to be displayed on the vehicle. The first plate, made of leather, was issued in 1906. It went to metal in 1910, porcelain in 1912 and tin in 1918. Plates became the responsibility of counties in 1911. The state took over registration in 1917, giving everyone two plates. People started getting one plate in 1922. During the Depression, stealing plates was common because people couldn't afford them. Beginning in 1963, tags were required for mobile homes, house trailers and campers.

Palm Beach Past: The Bust

In 1972, the state began allowing people to pick their own "vanity plate" number-letter combination for a twelve-dollar surcharge. In 1975, to cut costs, the state began issuing renewal decals instead of all-new plates. In 1978, Florida went to a mandatory alphanumeric system to allow for more combinations.

Some years ago when we first came to Florida, we noticed some cars with license plates with only the word "Seminole" on them. We were told they were issued to the Indians free. We no longer see them. What happened?
—Lee and Ed Hopke, Suburban Boynton Beach

They're still around. The plates are, in fact, distributed free and are issued directly by tag agencies of the Seminole and Miccosukee tribes, said Mary Jane Willie, clerk for the Seminole tribal tag agency in Hollywood.

The following are more fun facts about notations on license plates.

"Sunshine State" first appeared in 1949. A grapefruit in a corner, done in 1935, lasted only a year; it looked too much like a bomb. "Disabled veteran" started in 1951. That same year, a "Keep Florida Green" slogan was tried. It lasted only a year because some said it sounded like the state wanted all the tourists' money.

In 1957, "Horseless Carriage" was adopted for vehicles whose bodies and engines—not just kits—were at least thirty-five years old and which were driven for historical exhibitions. The 1965 tag marked the 400th anniversary of the first European encounter with Florida. "National Guard" was added that year as well. A wheelchair plate was added in 1974.

In the 1980s and 1990s, the state began adding notations such as "U.S. Reserve," "Ex-POW," "Pearl Harbor Survivor" and "Medal of Honor." The first specialty plate, to honor the *Challenger* astronauts, was issued in 1987. State universities followed that same year and private ones after that. The state also added such specialty plates as "Save the Manatee," "Florida Panther" and the controversial "Choose Life," which encourages adoption.

For more information, visit the Florida Department of Highway Safety and Motor Vehicles' website at www.hsmv.state.fl.us.

Originally published in the *Palm Beach Post*, October 30 and November 6, 2002.

Sources and Further Reading

The Death of Martin Tabert

Associated Press/*New York Times*, April 1–November 29, 1923.

Carper, N. Gordon. "Martin Tabert, Martyr of an Era." *Florida Historical Society Quarterly* (October 1973).

Rogers, Ken. "N.D. Man Flogged to Death." *Bismarck* [North Dakota] *Tribune*, November 24, 1997.

Wynne, Lewis N. "Prisoners and Public Opinion: Convict Lease System." Paper for the Florida Historical Society Annual Meeting, May 1996, Cocoa Beach.

The Ashley Gang

Archives of the *Palm Beach Post*, *Miami Metropolis*, *Tropical Sun*, *Miami Daily News*, *Miami News* and *Miami Herald*.

Historical Society of Palm Beach County

Stuart, Hix C. *The Notorious Ashley Gang*. Stuart, FL: St. Lucie Print Co., 1928.

Williams, Ada Coats. *Florida's Ashley Gang*. Port Salerno: Florida Classics Library, 1996.

Hypocrite's Row

Archives of the *Palm Beach Post*.
Tasker, Fred. "Rum Has Played a Crucial Part in New World's History." *Miami Herald*, August 8, 2000.

The Gulf Stream Pirate

Buchanan, Patricia. "Miami's Bootleg Boom." Tequesta (Historical Association of Southern Florida), 1970.
Caudle, Hal. *Hanging at Bahia Mar*. Historical Association of Southern Florida, n.d.
Crankshaw, Joe. "Finding God on Death Row an Old Story." *Miami Herald*, February 9, 1988.
Hollingsworth, Jodie. Audio interview. Fort Lauderdale Historical Society, August 25, 1962.
Records of the U.S. Coast Guard Board of Inquiry and U.S. District Court Trial. National Archives, Southeast Region, Morrow, Georgia.
Rowe, Sean. "The Gallows and the Deep." *New Times Broward–Palm Beach*, December 4, 1997.
U.S. Coast Guard archives.

Shootout on Old Dixxie

Archives of the *Palm Beach Post* and *New York Times*.
City of Lake Worth
Historical Societies of South Florida and Palm Beach County
Interviews with Robert Knox Moncure III and Margaret Moore Briant.
National Archives
Palm Beach County Court records.
Research assistance by Miami historian Paul George.
U.S. Bureau of Alcohol, Tobacco, Firearms and Explosives

Son of Al Capone

Auburn [California] *Journal*
London [England] *Daily Mail*

Miami Herald
Miami News
Palm Beach Post
Research assistance by Rebecca Smith, archivist, Historical Association of
  Southern Florida.

Hoagy in Palm Beach

Hoagy Carmichael Collection. Indiana University. www.dlib.indiana.edu/
  collections/hoagy.
Indiana Historical Society. www.indianahistory.org.

Gershwin in Palm Beach

Jablonski, Edward, and Lawrence D. Stewart. *The Gershwin Years*. Garden
  City, NY: Doubleday, 1973.
Kimball, Robert, and Alfred Simon. *The Gershwins*. New York: Atheneum,
  1973.
Schwartz, Charles. *Gershwin: His Life and Music*. Indianapolis: Bobs-Merrill
  Co., 1973.

First to Die in the Line of Duty

Wilbanks, William. *Forgotten Heroes: Police Officers Killed in Early Florida*.
  Paducah, KY: Turner Publishing Co., 1998.

The Pennocks

Snyder, James. *Five Thousand Years on the Loxahatchee*. Jupiter, FL: Pharos Books,
  2003.

Bill Boutwell: The Inventor of Half-and-Half

Mustaine, Beverly. *On Lake Worth*. Charleston, SC: Arcadia, 1999.

The WPA

Federal Writers' Project. *The WPA Guide to Florida*. New York: Pantheon Books, 1939. Reprint, 1984. [Both editions are out of print but may be available through used book stores or online book searches.]

The Campus Shop

Tuckwood, Jan, and Eliot Kleinberg. *Pioneers in Paradise*. Athens, GA: Longstreet Press, 2004.

About the Author

E liot Kleinberg is a native of Florida and author of a number of books about Florida history, including *Palm Beach Past: The Best of "Post Time."* He has been writing for the *Palm Beach Post* for over twenty years, and he is a member of the Palm Beach County Historical Society, the South Florida Historical Society and the Florida Historical Society. He lives in Boca Raton with his wife and two sons.

Visit us at
www.historypress.net